Tubrid Church of Ireland Graveyard, Drumkeeran Parish, County Fermanagh

by

David R. Elliott

Irish Genealogy Series

KinFolk Finders

Copyright 2025 David R. Elliott. All rights reserved.

This book is not to be copied or put into electronic format without the expressed written permission of KinFolk Finders.

David R. Elliott, Ph.D., M.Div., is the past-chair of the London & Middlesex Branch of the Ontario Genealogical Society and the founding vice-chair of the organization's Ireland Special Interest Group.

ISBN 978-1-927357-77-4

Cover photo is from Tubrid Graveyard (DRE 2016).

Additional copies can be obtained from:

KinFolk Finders
154 Main Street, Parkhill, Ontario,
Canada, N0M 2K0
Phone (519) 294-0728

We have photographs of all of the graves and their context in the cemetery. They can be purchased from **KinFolk Finders**.

Preface to the Irish Genealogy Series' New Format

When we first visited Ireland in 2004, we were searching for our Irish ancestors. We soon discovered that so many of its cemeteries had never been indexed. Those that had been done, were done poorly with only the most legible tombstones being recorded, and often the published indexes listed the stones alphabetically without any indication of their location or *in situ* context. Without detailed site maps, it was very difficult locating those stones. Taking our cue from the past cemetery indexing projects of the Ontario Genealogical Society, we felt that a better job could be done for Irish cemeteries.

The 1922 destruction of almost all of the pre-1901 Irish census records and the burning of most of the Church of Ireland (Anglican) parish registers, marriage bonds and wills in the explosion at the General Registry Office in Dublin during the civil war was a great tragedy. We are forced to use all sources available to us to recreate the past; information gained from cemeteries is thus very important.

Preface

With my background in archaeology, we have taken advantage of aerial photography and noting ground cover changes to detect buried stones, employing surveying techniques to map the cemeteries, using plain flour and water to highlight difficult texts, and creating digital photographic techniques to capture the images of hard-to-read inscriptions.

As a historian, I have sought to provide the most accurate reproduction of the information on the tombstones by checking questionable names, dates and ages against surviving parish registers, and civil registrations of births, marriages and deaths. In our transcriptions, we have provided the correct spellings of misspelled townlands, checking locations against the Tithe Applotments, the Griffith Valuation, and surviving census records. The name of the townland is so very important in Irish genealogical research.

In our research of each graveyard, we have keyed the transcriptions according to sections, rows and tombstone numbers to our maps of the cemeteries and their indexes. We have also recorded the spaces which may contain unmarked graves or unused plots. Every name on the tombstones has been recorded in the alphabetical comprehensive index at the back of each book.

Preface

For the Transcriptions of Tombstones section, we have employed various terms to describe the different types of grave markers. We have used the word plot to describe a defined burial area with four borders or different types of fences. Some have perimeter inscriptions on the curbs.

Some types of plots have only one border extending across their width and supports the headstone. We have called these partial plots.

There are various kinds of burial memorials found in the cemeteries. There are free-standing headstones, pedestal markers, temporary wooden crosses with plaques, flat stones, raised flats and sarcophagi (stone coffins above ground), also mausoleums and massive monuments. To help readers identify what we are describing, we have included a selection of different tombstone styles that we have encountered across Ireland.

Our own research and research for our clients has led us to index cemeteries in counties Antrim, Donegal, Fermanagh, Leitrim, Tyrone and also Wicklow. Initially our company, KinFolk Finders, published our indexes in-house, but we are now publishing them in a new format produced by Lightning Source in order to facilitate wider international exposure and ease of access. Eventually, all of our previous titles will be put into this new format. Some

Preface

smaller cemetery indexes will be consolidated with others in the same parish or pastoral charge.

For those who cannot personally visit these Irish cemeteries, we have put our photographs of each tombstone on FindmyPast.ie .

Contents

Preface to the Irish Genealogy Series' New Format.......iii

Table of Contents...1

Introduction... 3

Acknowledgements...5

Map of Counties in Ireland................................7

Map of Parishes in County Fermanagh.....................8

Map of Tubrid Area..9

Map of the Tubrid Graveyard............................10

Scenes of the Church and Graveyard.....................11

Bibliography..14

Tombstone styles...15

Transcriptions of Tombstones and Memorials 30

Key to Index of Names...................................75

Index of Names 77

Irish Genealogy Series Titles...........................95

Introduction

The Tubrid Church of Ireland (Anglican) graveyard is located to the north of the east end of Boa Island in Lower Lough Erne. It is in Drumkeeran Parish which was created out of Magheraculmoney Parish in 1770.

The correct name of the townland on which the graveyard sits is Tubbrid, but the name of the church has been shortened to Tubrid. The church was built in 1774 and is still in active use. We first walked this cemetery in 2005, but did not record it until July 2016. We have not added any new graves since 2016, but in 2024 we returned twice to the cemetery to clarify the inscriptions on some difficult tombstones and did retakes of some of the memorials inside the church. We also added another memorial that we had either missed or was added since 2016.

The oldest dateable tombstone is from 1842. The Church of Ireland burial register held by PRONI dates from 1836. (MIC1/37).

As we transcribed the inscriptions on the tombstones, we found that sometimes the names of the townlands were spelled incorrectly. We have corrected them to conform to the standard names set in 1851. Where we have changed the spelling, we have indicated it with an asterisk.*

Introduction

Because we are interested only in genealogical and historical information we have left out sayings, poems, scripture and supplications in our transcriptions.

There is only one marked grave in each of Sections A, B and E of the graveyard. The rows in Section C are irregular and crowded, with partial rows and Rows 5 and 7 splitting at their ends. We plotted the rows on our map as best we could. There are a lot of spaces which may contain unmarked graves.

Acknowledgements

We are grateful to Derek and Laura Elliott who graciously allowed us to use their cottage while we were working in Fermanagh. Later, David and Val Bailey were our gracious hosts while staying in our caravan at Blaney Caravan Park.

Special thanks goes to Brian Mitchell in Derry who granted permission for us to use and modify some of his parish maps from his *A New Genealogical Atlas of Ireland* published by Genealogical Publishing Co., Inc. in Baltimore.

Nancy Elliott recorded the tombstones while we surveyed the cemetery, and later prepared the maps. Linda Smith edited the manuscript.

Thanks goes to some members of the Select Vestry of the Tubrid church, who while preparing for the Vaughan Trust lecture in 2024 opened the church and allowed me to do photographic retakes of some of the memorials.

Acknowledgements

Blaney Caravan Park. New "shepherd hut" cabins. (DRE 2019).

Counties of Ireland

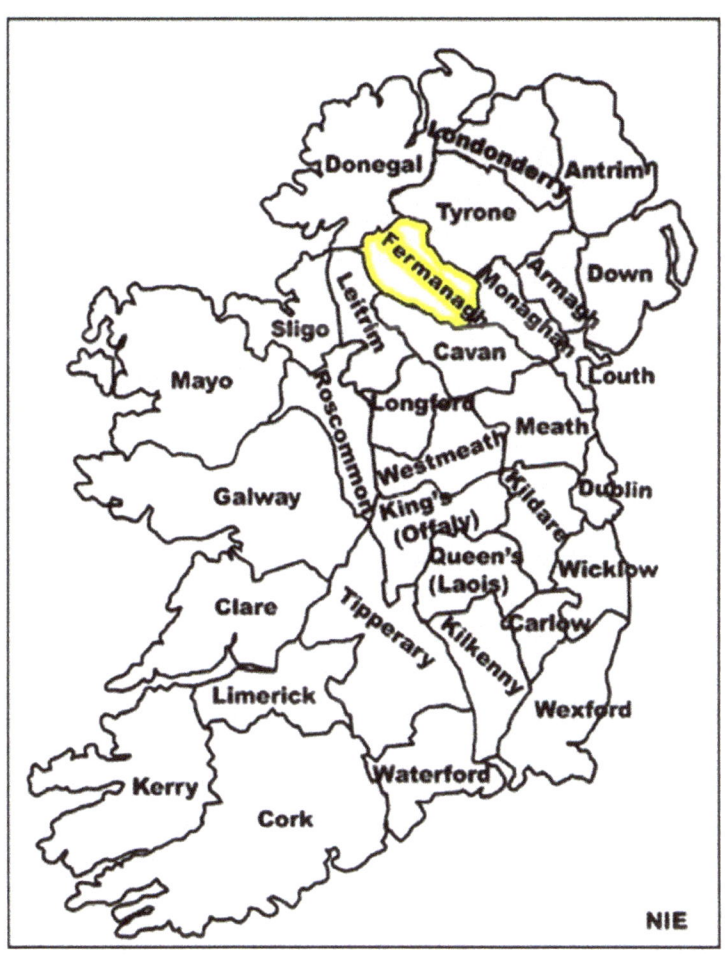

The six counties of Northern Ireland have a darker shading. Fermanagh is the most westerly of them. (NIE 2012).

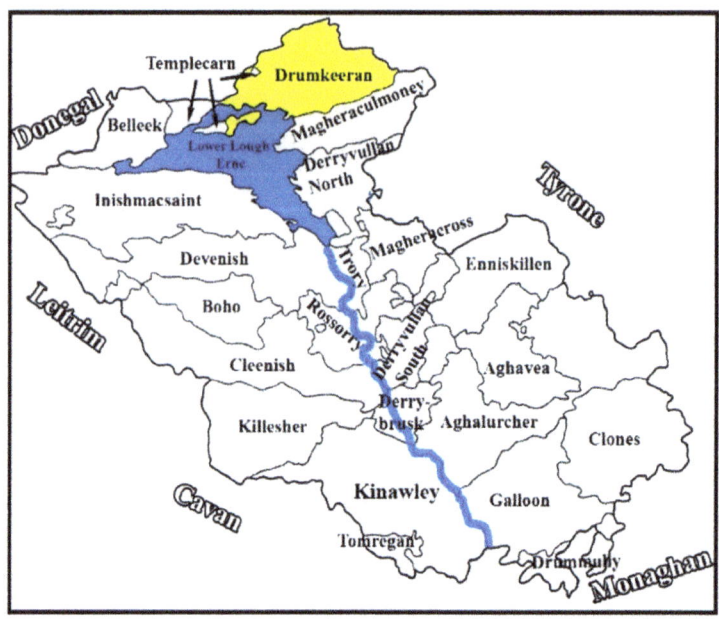

County Fermanagh parishes and the surrounding counties. (NIE 2024).

This is an approximate map of the parishes of County Fermanagh. It is very difficult to delineate the Upper Lough Erne on a map of this size because it is not a continuous large body of water, but a waterway interspersed with many islands. It is part of the Shannon River system that extends though the interior of Ireland. However, the Upper Lough Erne system becomes wider in places towards the southern border of the county. Drumkeeran Parish, featured in this book, is highlighted in yellow.

Tubrid Area

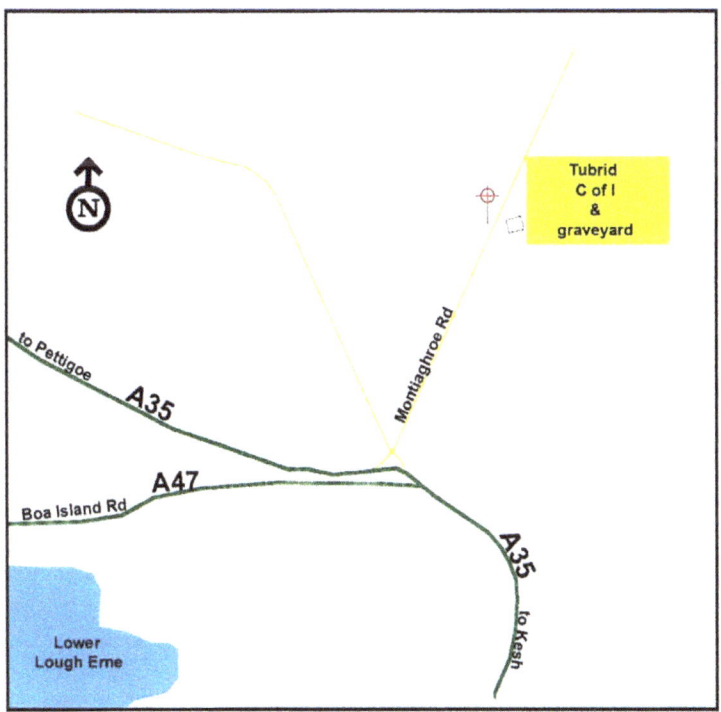

Tubrid Church of Ireland Graveyard on Montiagmore Road, across the road from church. (NIE 2016).

Map of Tubrid Graveyard

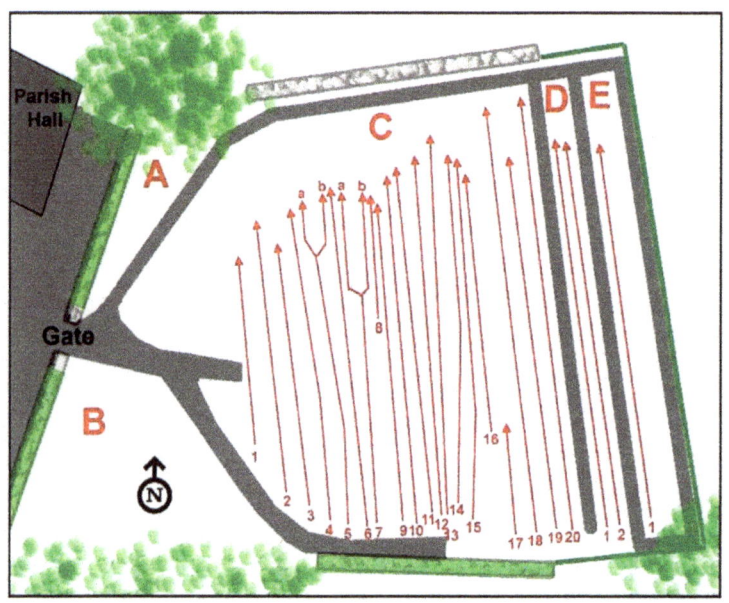

Tubrid Graveyard Map, showing irregular rows and partial rows. (NIE 2016).

Scenes of the Church and Graveyard

Tubrid Church of Ireland (DRE 2005).

Tubrid Graveyard is across the road from the church and behind the parish hall. Section C below. (DRE 2016).

Scenes

Part of Section C with Parish Hall in the background. (DRE 2016).

C1-1. Oldest dated tombstone in the graveyard from 1842. (DRE 2016).

Bibliography

Day, Angélique and Patrick McWilliams, eds. *Ordnance Survey Memoirs of Ireland Volume 14: Parishes of Co. Fermanagh II, 1834-5*. Belfast: Institute of Irish Studies, Queen's University, 1992.

Elliott, David R. *A Comprehensive Index of the St. Mary's Ardess Church of Ireland, Magheraculmoney Parish Registers, County Fermanagh, 1763-1918*. Parkhill: Kinfolk Finders, 2021.

Leslie, J.B., *et al. Clergy of Clogher*. Belfast: Ulster Historical Foundation, 2006.

Mitchell, Brian. *A New Genealogical Atlas of Ireland*, 2nd edition. Baltimore: Genealogical Publishing Co., Inc., 2002.

Styles of Tombstones

Plots

Plot: a burial area with four defined borders. (Fivemiletown, DRE 2024).

A fenced plot with a pillar headstone with inscriptions on all four sides. (Monea, DRE 2006).

Fenced plot with large funeral monument having architectural features. (Old Aghalurcher, DRE 2024).

Caged plot. (Monea, DRE 2023).

Partial plots with only one border, extending the full width of the burial area. (Colaghty, DRE 2023).

Flats

A large flat flagstone memorial. (Old Aghalurcher, DRE 2024).

Crested flat stone with herald crest above memorial text. (Old Aghalurcher, DRE 2024).

Raised flat or table monument with an inscription. (Garrison, DRE 2008).

Types of Headstones

Simple free-standing headstone. Older ones often have sunk into the ground, burying the lower rows of the inscriptions. (Monea, DRE 2006).

Tombstone Styles

Military marker erected by the Commonwealth War Graves Commission. (Benmore, DRE 2007).

Fancy children's burials. (Fivemiletown, DRE 2011).

Children's lot with toys. (Fivemiletown, DRE 2024).

High Celtic cross in a plot. (Ederney, DRE 2023).

Tombstone Styles

Stubby Celtic cross headstone. (Edenclaw, DRE 2023).

Roman cross headstone. (Edenclaw, DRE 2023).

Pedestal marker. (Garrison, DRE 2008).

Temporary wooden cross with plague. (Belcoo, DRE 2015).

Inscription on perimeter border of plot. (Derrbybrusk, DRE 2016).

Book-shaped marker. (Derrygonnelly, DRE 2009).

Inscribed flower holder; sometimes containing genealogical data. (Tubrid, DRE 2016).

Scroll-shaped headstones. (Derrybrusk, DRE 2016).

Sarcophagii

A sarcophagus is an above-ground stone coffin. (Benmore, DRE 2007).

Fancy low-profile sarcophagus. (Ballyshannon, DRE 2015).

Mausoleums

Mausoleums can be large above-ground burial structures or large underground rooms for the burials of wealthy families as below. (Aghavea, DRE 2012).

Mausoleum. (Ardess, DRE 2019).

Transcriptions of Tombstones

SECTION A

A1-1 [Raised flat]. Erected to the memory of the Revd. **James B. Tuttle**, A.B., J.P., who departed this life August 19th 1877, aged 90 yrs. He was 58 yrs. Rector of the Parish of Belleek.

SECTION B

B1-1 [**MORTON** partial plot]. In loving memory of **John**, died 9th August 1940, aged 75 yrs. His wife **Margaret** died 31st July 1967, aged 88 yrs. Their son **George** died 3rd July 1921, aged 6 yrs. And their grandson baby **Ivan Seaney**, died 2nd March 1945, aged 3 mths.

SECTION C

Row C1

C1-1 [Sunken headstone]. **A. Poster**, 1842.

Transcriptions

C1-2 [spaces].

C1-3 [Flat]. Sacred to the memory of **Jane Stedman** who departed this life on the 12th of February 1847, aged 70 years.

C1-4 [spaces].

C1-5 [Plot with white headstone]. Erected by **William** and **Phoebe Allen** in loving memory of their son **John**, who died 10th June 1900, aged 19 years. Their son **Samuel** died 11th Jan. 1916, aged 18 yrs. And his mother **Ellen** died 9th Jan. 1900, aged 96 yrs. Also their son **William** killed in France for King and Country, Sept. 9th 1916, aged 29 years. Also in memory of the above **William Allen** who died March 12th 1920, aged 70 years. His wife **Phoebe** died 12th June 1947, aged 92 years. Daughter-in-law **Emily** died 15th Dec. 1970, aged 75 years. Also their son **Christopher** died 1st Dec. 1989, aged 92 years.

Row C2

C2-1 [spaces].

C2-2 [Headstone]. In memory of **William Fitzpatrick**, died 17th March 1894. Also **Martha Fitzpatrick**, (16 years sextoness of Tubrid Church), died 15th July 1899.

Transcriptions

C2-3 [spaces].

C2-4 [Plot with headstone and low decorative metal fence; lead letters missing]. In loving memory of **Sarah Jane Richardson**, who with Christian resignation, passed away on 25th June 1898, in the 20th year of her age. Also **Charles Richardson** died 18th Dec. 1900, aged 19 years. And **Kate Richardson** died 14th Nov. 1901, aged 13 years.

C2-5 [**ARMSTRONG** plot with headstone and two perimeter inscriptions; oriented facing gate]. (Letterkeen, Kesh). In loving memory of **James**, died 4th May 1959, aged 70 years. His wife **Sarah Ann** died 17th November 1974, aged 70 years. Their son **Thomas William James (Jim)** died 15th April 1998, aged 58 years. [Perimeter]. 1. **Thomas** died 1st November 1932, aged 93 years. 2. **Catherine** died 1890.

C2-6 [space].

C2-7 [**ROBINSON** plot]. In loving memory of **William** who passed away 19th December 1986, aged 81 years. And his loving wife **Minnie** who passed away 28th February 1990, aged 74 years.

C2-8 [spaces].

C2-9 [Headstone]. **Henry Leonard**, 54 years Master of Tubrid School, died Nov. 16th 1875, aged 72 yrs.

C2-10 [spaces to end of row].

Transcriptions

ROW C3

C3-1 [spaces].

C3-2 [**GRIMSLEY** plot with flower holder inscribed on four sides]. **William** died 20th Oct. 1959, aged 73. Wife **Elizabeth** died 19th July 1972, age 86 years. Daughter **Annie** died 18th June 1993, aged 69 years. Son **William** died 22nd June 1980, aged 77 years.

C3-3 [**THOMPSON** plot with headstone and military marker]. In loving memory of **Frank Thompson** (Bannagh Beg*), died 9th Nov. 1908, aged 12 years. Also his mother **Elizabeth Thompson** died 14th Dec. 1946, aged 75 years. Also her husband **George Thompson** died 29th May 1959, aged 86 years. [Military marker]. 14434065 Private **B.H. Sims**, The Seaforth Highlanders, 8th July 1946. [CWGC lists him as **Barton Hugh Sims**].

C3-4 [**THOMPSON** headstone]. In loving memory of **Rose** and **Isaac Thompson**, their daughter **Mary Simms** and their son **George**.

C3-5 [spaces with mounds].

C3-6 [**BARTON** plot; no other identification].

C3-7 [small space].

C3-8 [**GIBSON** plot with two perimeter inscriptions]. In loving memory of **William Gibson** (Tubrid), died 12th July 1949, aged 58 years. Also his wife **Margaret** died 26th

April 1964, aged 73 years. [Perimeter]. **Emily Gibson** died 13th August 1980. **Frederick Gibson** died 9th July 1984.

C3-9 [Plot with low horizontal iron railing]. In loving memory of **John Barton**, died Sept. 1907. His wife **Rebecca** died June 1920. Their son **William Barton** died 11th April 1921, aged 59 years. Aunt **Eliza Reid** died Dec. 1906. Erected by their daughter **Sarah Barton**.

C3-10 [Broken headstone]. In loving memory of **Joe McCormick** of Crillan* who died May 1st 1907, aged 84. Also his wife **Bessie McCormick** who died Aug. 13th 1916, aged 97 years.

C3-11 [spaces].

C3-12 [Plot]. In loving memory of **James Thompson** (Edenticromman*). His wife **Elizabeth** and daughter **Sarah Jane**. Son **James** died 31st Dec. 1982.

C3-13 [spaces to end of row].

ROW C4

C4-1 [spaces].

C4-2 [**KEYS** plot]. In loving memory of a dear husband and father. **Robert** died 28th November 1972, aged 56 years. Also wife and mother **Lilian** died 4th December 1996, aged 75 years.

Transcriptions

C4-3 [**SEANEY** plot]. In loving memory of **John (Jack) Seaney** (Rosscolban*), died 23rd July 1967, aged 59 years. Also his wife **Sarah (Sadie)** died 25th May 1992, aged 77 years.

C4-4 [**ARMSTRONG** plot with plaque; no other details]. (Drumrush).

C4-5 [spaces].

C4-6 [Plot with tall headstone and low iron railing]. In loving memory of **Thomas Stewart** of Bannagh* Lodge, who died 3rd August 1907, aged 60 years. And of **Jane Stewart**, his wife, who died 8th April 1911, aged 65 years. Also of their daughter **Kate Louisa Stewart** who died 11th January 1926, aged 48 years.

C4-7 [Plot with tall headstone; some lead letters missing]. In loving memory of **Barbara Ogle** (Drumrush) who died 12th Nov. 1910, aged 59 years. Also her husband **George** died 25th March 1930, aged 93 years. **Elizabeth**, wife of **Adam**, died 9th March 1932, aged 42 years. Also **Adam Ogle** died 10th October 1975, aged 91 years. **Gladys Evelyn Ogle** died 14th October 2002, aged 86 years.

C4-8 [space].

C4-9 [**McCLELLAND** plot]. In loving memory of **Edward**, died 9th May 1935, aged 63 years. Also his wife **Isabella** died 14th November 1952, aged 81 years. And their daughter **Elizabeth Annabella** died 12th January 1968, aged 63 years.

Transcriptions

C4-10 [spaces and mounds].

C4-11 [**VANCE** headstone; no other details].

C4-12 [spaces and mounds to end of row].

ROW C5

C5-1 [small space].

C5-2 [**THOMPSON** plot]. In loving memory of a dear husband and father. **Cecil** departed this life 14th June 1978. Wife and mother **Martha** departed this life 27th June 1990.

C5-3 [**ARMSTRONG** plot]. In loving memory of our dear father **Johnston Armstrong** who passed away 8th March 1968. And of our beloved mother **Mary** who passed away 14th April 1970. Also their son **John Alexander (Jack)** who passed away 1st October 2014.

C5-4 [Plot with scroll-style headstone]. In loving memory of **Mary Elizabeth Frazer** (Letterkeen), died 5th Feb. 1967, aged 39 years. Also daughter **Isobel** died 3rd Nov. 1967, aged 6 years. Also her father **Samuel Albert** died 17th Sept. 1985, aged 72 years.

C5-5 [**KIDNEY** plot]. In loving memory of **Elizabeth**, died 19th January 1966, aged 67 years. Also her husband **Richard** died 12th December 1966, aged 74 years. And their son **Thomas J.** died 20th April 1969, aged 42 years.

Transcriptions

C5-6 [**ARMSTRONG** plot]. (Bannagh Beg*).

C5-7 [**WALMSLEY** plot]. In loving memory of **John Walmsley**, J.P., died 14th April 1952. His wife **May** died 11th December 1961. Their son **Herbert** died 8th January 2014.

C5-8 [**GRAHAM** plot]. In memory of a loving wife and devoted mother **Evelyn**, died 2nd November 1971, aged 42 years. **Helena Graham** died 20th September 1942. Her husband **John Graham** died 4th March 1966. Also their son **William John Graham**, beloved husband of **Evelyn**, died 9th July 2000, aged 77 years.

C5-9 [**BRIMSTONE** plot]. In loving memory of **James Andrew**, died 7th February 1941, aged 14 years. His mother **Mary W.W.** died 28th October 1975, aged 81 years. His father **James Alexander** died 16th July 1983, aged 88 years. His sister **C. Joyce Kennedy** died 14th May 2004, aged 72 years.

C5-10 [Plot]. In loving memory of **George Armstrong** (Mullanmeen*), died 9th March 1941, aged 83 years. Also his wife **Elizabeth Armstrong**, died 18th March 1956, aged 80 years. Also their son **John** died 27th Sept. 1972, aged 73 years. Also **Isobel** died 30th Jan. 1962, aged 54 years. And **Alexander** died 13th Nov. 1963, aged 60 years.

C5-11 [space].

C5-12 [Plot]. The **GILMORE** Family and **LEWTHWAITE** Family.

C5-13 [spaces and mounds].

[Row 5 splits].

C5-14A [**THOMPSON** plot with plaque and flower holder]. In loving memory of our parents **Jack** and **Catherine**. [Flower holder]. **John Thompson**.

C5-14B [**JOHNSTON** plot]. (Mullanmeen*). In loving memory of **George**, died 5th February 1967, aged 74 years. Also his wife **Catherine** died 25th October 1973, aged 80 years. **Robert H. Martin** (Innisclin) died 25th June 1984, aged 84 years. **William James** died December 2004, aged 72 years. [It is unclear whether the latter person was a Johnston or a Martin. We have listed him in the index as a Johnston].

C5-15 [spaces to end of row].

ROW C6

C6-1 [space].

C6-2 [Small plot]. Beloved babies of **Victor** and **Irene Thompson**.

C6-3 [spaces].

Transcriptions

C6-4 [**MARTIN** plot with columned headstone]. In loving memory of our dear grandparents and parents: **William John (Willie)** who died on 3-4-1965, aged 87. And his beloved wife **Jane** who died on 20-4-1969, aged 85. And their son **Robert Henry (Bob)** who died on 30-7-2005, aged 81. And his beloved wife **Maud Evelyn** who died on 20-2-2007, aged 79.

C6-5 [Plot]. In loving memory of my dear parents: **Alice Johnston** died 9th Oct. 1956, aged 71 years. **James Johnston** died 3rd Dec. 1964, aged 83 years.

C6-6 [spaces].

C6-7 [**MORTON** plot with two perimeter inscriptions; difficult to read because of grey granite]. **Christina Jane Morton** died 18th Nov. 1968, aged 43 years. **William Morton** died [...] 1979, aged 68 years.

C6-8 [Plot]. In loving memory of my dear wife **Letitia Woods**, died 29th March 1988. Also **William Henry Woods** died 18th December 1977.

C6-9 [spaces].

C6-10 [**BROWN** plot; grey granite headstone with *bas* relief lettering; difficult to read. Date for **Mary** should be 1957, aged 81.] In loving memory of **Mary Annabella Brown** who died 30th March 1958 [*sic*], aged 83 [*sic*] years. Also her husband **James** who died 22nd March 1966, aged 94 years. Also their son **Thomas** who died 18th Dec. 1966, aged 56 years.

C6-11 [space].

C6-12 [**JOHNSTON** plot; no details].

C6-13 [space].

C6-14 [**BARTON** plot]. (Mullanmeen*). In loving memory of **Isabella**, died 17th August 1959, aged 66 years. Also her husband **Adam** died 21st July 1973, aged 84 years.

C6-15 [spaces to the end of row].

ROW C7

C7-1 [space].

C7-2 [**ARMSTRONG** plot]. In loving memory of **Susanna Armstrong** (Dooraa* North), died 24th August 1971, aged 92 years. Also her daughter **Edith Maud**, died 14th March 1998, aged 86 years. And her son **William John** died 2nd March 2006, aged 88 years.

C7-3 [**MORROW** plot]. In loving memory of **Margaret Sarah Barbara**, died 11th April 1963. Her husband **William Henry** died 28th April 1963. Their son **John James** died 15th August 1986. And his wife **Evelyn Mary** died 28th February 1974.

C7-4 [spaces with mounds].

C7-5 [Plot with headstone]. The **AIKEN** Family (Killygarry, Ederney).

C7-6 [space].

C7-7 [**MARSHALL** plot with headstone and inscribed flower holder]. In loving memory of **Herbert**, died 9th October 1988. Also his brother **Alfred** died 3rd January 1997. And **Evelyn**, wife of **Herbert**, died 2nd September 2007, aged 73 years. [Flower holder]. **Mary Jane** died 6th May 1961, aged 77 years.

C7-8 [**MARSHALL** plot with headstone and flower holder]. In loving memory of a dear husband, father and grandfather: **Ernest** died 19th November 1987, aged 70 years. [Flower holder]. **Ernest J. Marshall**.

C7-9 [Plot; much of the inscription under glass is missing; dates from civil registrations]. In loving memory of **Martha Barton** (Clonelly) who died 24th June 1940, aged 76 years. Also **John Barton** (Clonelly) who died February [11th 1943], aged [85] years.

C7-10 [**MOORE** plot]. In loving memory of **Rebecca Moore**, died 8th June 1933. And her husband **Robert** died 4th February 1906. Their daughter **Daisy** died 10th September 1981. Their son **James** died 2nd July 1984. Their grand-daughter **Sandra** died 12th November 1982. Their daughter-in-law **Mary** died 31st July 1988. Also their son **Samuel Crawford (Sam)** died 4th March 1993.

C7-11 [spaces and mounds].

Transcriptions

C7-12 [**ROBINSON** plot with five perimeter inscriptions]. **Edward John** died 16th September 1938. **Olive Lucy** died 21st March 1975. **Samuel George** died 1st February 1986. Infant son **Brian** died 5th November 1945. **Vivien Maud** died 4th November 1974.

[Row splits].

C7-13A [plot]. In loving memory of **Sarah,** the beloved wife of **Henry Humphries**, who died 17th February 1944, aged 66 years.

C7-13B [Plot with no identification].

C7-14A [spaces to end of row].

C7-14B [**LENNOX** plot; no details].

C7-15B [**FARRELL** base for headstone; no other details].

C7-16 [spaces to end of row].

ROW C8 [Partial Row starting half way down].

C8-1 [**THOMPSON** plot]. In loving memory of **Thomas Charles**, died 6th April 1952, aged 72 years. His wife **Elizabeth** died 13th March 1968, aged 81 years. Their son **William John** died 28th March 1998, aged 79 years. And his wife **Evelyn** died 26th March 1979, aged 55 years.

C8-2 [spaces and mounds].

Transcriptions

C8-3 [**ARMSTRONG** headstone]. In loving memory of **James**, died 2nd August 1944. His wife **Isabella** died 19th October 1951. Their son **James** died 4th September 1963. His wife **May** died 19th June 1990. Their great-grandson **Colin** died 27th July 1970. Also their baby son.

C8-4 [**FARRELL** flower holder].

C8-5 [spaces to end of row].

ROW C9

C9-1 [Long space with mounds].

C9-2 [old headstone; no lettering].

C9-3 [space].

C9-4 [**WALMSLEY** plot]. In loving memory of **Margaret Walmsley** (Corlave), died 14th April 1944, aged 70 years. Also **Sarah Anne**, wife of **Edward Walmsley**, died 4th Feby. 1946, aged 45 years. And **Edward Walmsley** died 24th April 1959, aged 89 years. Also **Sheila Walmsley** died 1st Dec. 2002, aged 67 years. And **William Walmsley**, husband of **Sheila**, died 10th May 2011, aged 82 years.

C9-5 [space].

C9-6 [**WILSON** plot; no other details].

C9-7 **[WILSON** plot]. In loving memory of **Charles Wilson**, died 8th July 1974, aged 83 years. And **Elizabeth** died 22nd April 1932, aged 49 years. His infant grandson **Raymond Charles** died 19th Jan. 1967. And **Catherine** died 14th April 1989, aged 89 years. Son **Robert John** died 10th May 1998, aged 63 years. **Mervyn James**, son of above **Robert John**, died 29th March 2004, aged 45 years.

C9-8 **[BRANDON** plot with perimeter inscriptions]. **Mary Brandon** died 9th May 1934. **John Brandon** died 16th Feb. 1932. **Elizabeth Brandon** died 18th June 1990. **William Brandon** died 19th March 1989.

C9-9 **[CHITTICK** plot]. In loving memory of **Annie**, died 14th Nov. 1929, aged 69 years. Her husband **George** died 7th May 1939, aged 93 years. Their son **George** died 10th Oct. 1942, aged 46 years. **Elizabeth Jane Chittick** died 30th Jany. 1974, aged 64 years. Her husband **John Henry** died 11th Aug. 1978, aged 83 years. Their son **George Alexander** died 14th Feb. 1986, aged 43 years.

C9-10 [caged mass of lilies; uncertain about who is buried there].

C9-11 [Plot]. In memory of **William Johnston** (Lettercran [Donegal]) died 21st Jan. 1922, aged 70. Also his wife **Jane** died 10th Aug. 1933, aged 80. And **Margaret**, beloved wife of **Wm. Johnston** (Skea), died 28th April 1934, aged 30.

C9-12 [**FRAZER** headstone]. In loving memory of **Alexander Frazer** (Muckross), died 29th March 1935. Also his wife **Margaret** died 31st March 1958. And their daughter **Rebecca Forde** died 4th May 1933. Also their son **Irvine** died 8th Nov. 1943. Also their son **William Henry** died 31st Oct. 1966. And their son **James** died 19th December 1984, aged 79 years.

C9-13 [**MILLS** plot]. In loving memory of **Joseph**, died 28th July 1968. His wife **Mary** died 29th May 1976. And their son **William** died 24th March 1994. Also his wife **Dora** died 1st January 2010.

C9-14 [spaces to end of row].

ROW C10

C10-1 [space].

C10-2 [small grave with flower holder indicating it was for a person's husband].

C10-3 [spaces].

C10-4 [**ALLEN** plot with flower holder]. **Lizzie Swindall**, 1914-1985, beloved mother, U.S.A.

C10-5 [space].

C10-6 [**McCARTNEY** plot]. In loving memory of **Alfred McCartney**, died 3rd June 1935, aged 8 years. Also his

Transcriptions

father **Edward McCartney** died 16th September 1976, aged 86 years. His mother **Margaret Ellen** died 11th Jan. 1986, aged 81 years. Also their son **Samuel Edward** died 7th December 2010, aged 80 years.

C10-7 [Broken headstone]. In memory of **George Allingham**, died 15th Oct. 1931. His wife **Catherine** died 8th March 1932. From their loving daughter **Emily** (Scotland).

C10-8 [spaces].

C10-9 [Plot]. In loving memory of **William Swanston**, died 16th March 1930, aged 86 years. His wife **Ann Jane** died 28th December 1945, aged 87 years. Also their granddaughter **Elizabeth Jane** died 9th Sept. 1931, aged 26 years.

C10-10 [**MOORE** plot]. In loving memory of **James Moore** (Drumnagalliagh), died 22nd October 1929. His wife **Elizabeth** died 29th December 1953. **Mervyn Alexander Moore** died 28th March 1946. **Isabella K. Moore** died 28th October 1973. Her husband **James Moore** died 11th May 1986.

C10-11 [Large family plot taking up rows 10-11; tree shaped pink granite headstone inscribed on two sides]. In loving memory of **Robert Edward Johnston** (Letterkeen), who died 5th April 1923, aged 22 years. His sister **Martha Jean** died 2nd February 1931, aged 23 years. His sister **Henrietta Mary** died 27th March 1937, aged 33 years. His mother **Nancy** died 29th Sept. 1943, aged 76 years. His father **George** died 6th Sept. 1950, aged 80 years. Daughter **Eva** died 2nd March 1979, aged 68 years. [Side Two]. In loving memory of **Mary Jane Johnston** (Meenmore) who died 21st Dec. 1920, aged 76 years. And her husband **James Johnston** who died 7th Jan. 1925, aged 86 years. His grandson **Richard James** died 15th Dec. 1980, aged 81 years. And his wife **Elizabeth Jane** died 22nd June 1979, aged 78 years. Their grandson **John Hargreaves** died 15th Sept. 1985, aged 80 years. And great grandson **James Robert** died 10th Aug. 1985, aged 46 years. [It is presumed that the latter person was a Hargreaves].

C10-12 [**STEVENSON** plot]. In loving memory of **Edward Stevenson**, died 28th March 1933, aged 84. His wife **Martha Jane** died 22nd March 1936, aged 79. Their daughter **Dora** died 26th Feb. 1924, aged 26. Their son **William John** died 8th April 1975, aged 84. And his wife **Susan** died 16th Jan. 1972, aged 70.

[Row ends with large plant].

ROW C11

C11-1 [spaces].

C11-2 [flower holder; no identification].

C11-3 [spaces and mounts].

C11-4 [**SPENCE** plot with two headstones facing each other]. In loving memory of **Robert L. Spence** (Clonelly), who died 14th February 1932, aged 39. **Rebecca Spence** 27th Nov. 1938. **Ethel Spence** 14th March 1959. **James Spence** 22nd June 1959. [Headstone 2]. In loving memory of **Robert C. Dundas**, died 25th Sept. 1937. Also his wife **Edith M. Dundas** died 25th Jany. 1961.

C11-5 [spaces and mounds].

C11-6 [extension of C10-11].

C11-7 [Plot with tall headstone]. Erected by **Wm. J.** and **Rebecca McCartney** (Skea) in memory of their dear father **Johnston McCartney** who died 14th March 1921, aged 77 years. Also our dear mother **Letitia** who died 1st Sept. 1925, aged 83 years. Also the above named **William James** who died 11th Jan. 1941, aged 72 years. And **Rebecca** who died 15th Oct. 1948, aged 76 years. Also **Sarah Johnston** who died 18th Dec. 1948, aged 74 years.

C11-8 [Headstone; some lead letters missing]. In loving memory of **Thomas McCutcheon** (Gortnaree) who died 18th March 1924, aged 99 years. Also of his wife **Margaret**, died 24th February 1929, aged 90 years. And of **Charles McCutcheon**, died 14th Oct. 1936, aged 74 years. And his wife **Eliza Jane**, died 17th November 1964, aged 82 years.

Transcriptions

C11-9 [Plot]. The Burying Ground of the **JOHNSTON** Family (Stragolan).

C11-10 [spaces and mounds].

C11-11 [Plaque belonging to broken **MARSHALL** headstone from plot C12-10 immediately behind it]. (Drumbrick). **John** died 1st March 1958. **Isobell** died 10th July 1969. **Annie** died 5th November 1978.

C11-12 [mound with large fern].

C11-13 [spaces and mounds].

C11-14 [**SPROULE** plot]. In loving memory of a devoted husband and father, **Robert** passed away 1st May 1988, aged 81 years. And a loving wife and mother, **Mildred** passed away 18th October 1998, aged 77 years.

C11-15 [**THOMPSON** plot with headstone and book-shaped memorial]. In loving memory of a devoted husband, father and grandfather, **Thomas Edward (Eddie)**, died 16th June 2013, aged 88 years. [Memorial]. Love: **Elsie, Helen, Brian, Linda, Trevor, Sandra** and families.

ROW C12

C12-1 [spaces].

C12-2 [plot with no identification].

C12-3 [Plot with low iron rails and tall headstone]. In loving memory of **Sidney Aiken**, died 8th May 1920, aged 72 years. And of **Esther Aiken**, died 18th May 1921, aged 78 years. Daughters of the late **Thomas Aiken** (Greaghmore).

C12-4 [spaces with mounds].

C12-5 [Plot with low iron railing and small headstone]. Erected to the cherished memory of two dearly beloved aunts: **Sidney Allingham** (Boa Island), who departed this life 21st March 1917, aged 85 years. And **Frances Allingham**, her sister, 7th March 1919, aged 96 years. And of dearest mother **Elizabeth Jane Allingham** who fell asleep 23rd April 1928, aged 84 years. **Frances Jane** 1874-1945. **Mary Alice** 1884-1956. **Charlotte Elizabeth** 1880-1956.

C12-6 [Large plot with tall headstone and perimeter inscriptions]. In loving memory of **Ann Barton** who died 13th April 1910 at Clonelly, Co. Fermanagh. Also **Thomas Barton** who died 1st January 1898 at Clonelly, Murga, Australia. Erected by their son and daughter. Also **Henry George Hart** who died 8th Feb. 1964. His wife **Margaret Hart** died 29th Nov. 1979. And their son **William Folliott Hart** died 9th Sept. 2010. [Perimeter]. **Folliott Warren Barton**, D.L., J.P., of Clonelly, died 27th March 1922. **John Huston Fraser** of Sydney, Australia, died 20th March 1926. **Margaret D. Barton** died 29th November 1944.

Transcriptions

C12-7 [**FITZPATRICK** plot]. In loving memory of **Susan** (Clonaweel, Kesh), died 25th July 1954, aged 85 yrs. **William James** died 12th March 1958, aged 60 yrs. **Alexander** (Winnipeg, Manitoba, Canada), died 24th May 1986, aged 82 yrs.

C12-8 [Headstone with some lead letters missing]. In loving memory of **Thomas Chittick** (Rotten Mountain*), who died 11th May 1910, aged 90 years. Also his wife **Christianna** who died 29th May 1910, aged 80 years.

C12-9 [Plot]. In loving memory of my dear husband **Irvine Armstrong** (Letterkeen), who fell asleep in Jesus 7th June 1912, aged 65 years. Also his wife **Susan Armstrong** died April 11th 1918, aged 79 years. Also **Irvine Armstrong** died 31st July 1965, aged 71 years.

C12-10 [Plot with two headstones; the second headstone is broken and lying behind in Row C11-11]. In loving memory of the **MARSHALL** family. (Drumbrick).

C12-11 [mound with fern].

C12-12 [**DICK** plot]. In loving memory of **Rachel Jane Dick**, died 26th Sept. 1935. Also her loving husband **Christopher**, died 24th Feb. 1955. Their daughter **Kathleen Mildred** died 24th Dec. 1980. Their son **William John** died 2nd July 2000.

C12-13 [**McCREA** plot]. (Dromore Little). **George** died 9th April 1941. His wife **Mary Jane** died 22nd November 1968.

C12-14 [spaces to end of row].

ROWC13

C13-1 [spaces].

C13-2 [**BELL** plot]. In loving memory of my dear husband **Willie**, died 18th August 1972, aged 69 yrs. His brother **Thomas** died 4th November 1992, aged 75 yrs. Their mother **Mary Ann** died 31st October 1974, aged 98 yrs.

C13-3 [space].

C13-4 [**READ** flower holder; no details].

C13-5 [space].

C13-6 [Large plot]. In loving memory of **George Barton** (Bannagh More*), died 29th August 1942, aged 77 years. And his beloved wife **Sarah Jane** died 1st April 1957, aged 85 years. Also their son **George** died 24th February 1967, aged 60 years. Also **Harry** died 27th December 1982, aged 72 years.

C13-7 [**CHITTICK** plot]. In loving memory of our dear parents: **Elizabeth J.** died 19th Nov. 1928, aged 40 years. **William** died 4th Feb. 1961, aged 85 years. And their son **William Sampson Chittick** died 22nd August 1980, cremated in Bedford, England. And son **Archibald** died 19th January 1997.

Transcriptions

C13-8 [space].

C13-9 [**STEVENSON** partial plot]. (Rotten Mountain). In loving memory of our mother **Margaret Jane (Maggie)**, died 25th February 1955, aged 38 years. Also our brother **James** died in infancy. And our grandparents: **Mary Ann (Minnie)** died 18th May 1945, aged 69 years. **John Thomas (Tom)** died 29th December 1951, aged 75 years.

C13-10 [**MOORE** plot]. In loving memory of **William** who died 8th July 1979, aged 70 years. His wife **Anna Elizabeth** who died 4th December 1989, aged 76 years.

C13-11 [**KNOX** plot]. In loving memory of my dear wife **Evelyn Knox** (Dernashesk*), died 31st March 1972, age 49 years. Also her husband **Matthew Henry** died 7th July 1979, age 68 years.

C13-12 [space].

C13-13 [Plot with **McCLELLAND** flower holder].

C13-14 [space with mound].

C13-15 [Plot with tree trunk style headstone]. In loving memory of **Annie Armstrong** who died 28th Sept. 1922, aged 58 years. In memory of **Isabella Armstrong** (Drumrush), died 22nd June 1934, age 60. **Henry Armstrong** died 12th March 1933, age 67. And his son **William James Armstrong** died 1st Oct. 1979, age 79. Also his wife **Faith Armstrong** died 30th April 1981, age 82.

Transcriptions

C13-16 [space].

C13-17 [plot; no identification].

C13-18 [**CUTHBERTSON** partial plot]. In loving memory of **William** 1928-1929. **Jane** 1859-1929. **William** 1857-1943. **Elizabeth** 1896-1974. **Robert** 1893-1979.

C13-19 [**CUTHERTSON** headstone]. In loving memory of **John**, died 10th Sept. 1929, aged 48 years. His wife **Frances** (*nee* **Fyffe**) died 10th Oct. 1942, aged 52 years. Their son **Andrew** died 22nd July 1944, aged 25 years.

C13-20 [spaces and mounds to end of row].

ROW C14

C14-1 [spaces].

C14-2 [**JOHNSTON** plot]. In fond remembrance of **George Johnston** (Drumcurren*), died 18th May 1979.

C14-3 [spaces and mounds].

C14-4 [Plot with badly stained **MOORE** headstone]. In sacred memory of **Charles Moore** (Drumkeeran House), who died 21st July 1917, aged 65 years. [Civil registration of death has age 60]. **Elizabeth Gibson Moore** died 8th June 1927, aged 65 years. And their children: **Henrietta** died 16th Aug. 1934, aged 40 years. **William** died 10th Sep.

Transcriptions

1962, aged 74 years. **Sarah** died 31st Jan. 1963, aged 72 years.

C14-5 [Plot with headstone and perimeter inscription]. In loving memory of **Sarah Marshall** (Drumchorick*), died 20th Aug. 1929, aged 69 years. And her children: **Mary** died 20th April 1901, aged 14 years. **Edward** died 1st March 1919, aged 26 years. Also her husband **John** died 17th Jan. 1932, aged 86 years. And their grandchildren: **Olive** died 1st May 1941, aged 3 months. **Muriel** died 6th Oct. 1942, aged 3 years. **Henry Marshall** died 10th Nov. 1979, aged 81 years. **George Marshall** died 14th Feb. 1985, aged 90 years. **Isaballa Margaret**, wife of **Henry**, died 23rd Oct. 2002, aged 87 years. [Perimeter]. **Martha Elizabeth** died 4th Sept. 1978, aged 48 years.

C14-6 [mound and space].

C14-7 [**JOHNSTON** plot; no other details].

C14-8 [**LOANE** plot]. In loving memory of our dear son **Earnest Carson Loane** who died 19th Nov. 1920, aged 12 years. **William Loane** died 26 Nov. 1934, aged 67 years. **Christopher Loane** died 1st February 1952, aged 49. **Sarah Jane**, wife of **Wm. Loane**, died 20th Nov. 1957, aged 79 years. Their daughter **Kathleen** died 9th Feb. 1979, aged 68 years. Her brother **John** died 5th January 1983, aged 78 years.

C14-9 [space].

C14-10 [Plot]. In loving memory of **Sidney Boyd** (Corlave), who died 21st June 1921, aged 56 years. Also her husband **John Boyd** died 14th Jan. 1945, aged 75. Also grandson **Irvine** died 28th Dec. 1972, aged 21 yrs. Also his parents: **Annie** died 7th Jan. 1984, aged 68 yrs. **Thomas** died 22nd Jan. 1984, aged 74 yrs.

C14-11 [spaces and mounds to end of row].

ROW C15

C15-1 [many spaces].

C15-2 [**LOANE** plot]. In fond memories of **Irvine**, died 30th December 1960. His wife **Elizabeth Mary** died 27th October 1976. Also their son **James** died 22nd December 1985.

C15-3 [space with mound].

C15-4 [Headstone]. Mother. In loving memory of **Maria H. Taggart** who died 4th February 1915, aged 52 years. **Samuel Taggart** who died 10th February 1969. **Alexander Taggart Benjamin Noble** 17-6-1937 [to] 26-4-1940. **Benjamin Laurence Noble**, son of **Jean Noble**, 9-9-1947 [to] 23-12-1947 (Grouselodge).

C15-5 [space].

C15-6 [Plot]. In loving memory of **Hiram Duffy** (Bannagh*) who died 15th Feby. 1918, aged 89 years. Also his wife **Frances** who died 6th May 1915, aged 57 years. And his sister **Elizabeth Anderson** who died 14th Feby. 1925, aged 85 years. And his brother-in-law **Robert Duffy** who died 11th October 1944, aged 73 years. Also his son **William John** who died 31st July 1971, aged 72 years. And his daughter **Elizabeth** who died 8th March 1974, aged 82 years. Also his daughter **Mary Jane** who died 16th July 1975, aged 80 years.

C15-7 [space].

C15-8 [Plot; some lead letters missing on headstone]. In loving memory of my dear parents: **Mary McCormick** who died 27th Jan. 1925. Also her husband **David** who died 31st Oct. 1937. And their daughter **Rose** who died 30th Jan. 1919. Erected by their daughter **Elizabeth McCormick**.

C15-9 [Pink granite tree trunk shaped headstone]. In loving memory of my dear husband **Robert McCutcheon** (Skea), who died 21st January 1918, aged 57 years.

C15-10 [**McCUTCHEON** headstone]. In loving memory of **John McCutcheon** (Movarran*), who died 25th December 1936, aged 74 years. And his wife **Elizabeth Jane** who died 20th January 1967, aged 94 years.

C15-11 [spaces and mounds].

C15-12 [**BOYD** plot with perimeter inscription]. **Sadie** died 7th November 1984.

Transcriptions

C15-13 [Headstone]. In loving memory of **William Johnston** who died 16th March 1920, aged 83 yrs. Also his wife **Sarah** who died 14th Feb. 1914, aged 79 years. Erected by their son **James**.

C15-14 [spaces and mounds].

C15-15 [Headstone]. In memory of **William John Beatty** of Dernashesk*, who died 8th July 1921. Also his brother **James** who died 14th August 1915.

C15-16 [spaces].

C15-17 [plot with cement headstone; no identification].

C15-18 [**BROWN** plot with two perimeter inscriptions]. **James Frederick** died 10th Nov. 1986. **Maud Elizabeth** died 10th Feb. 2007.

C15-19 [Plot]. In loving memory of **Louisa Irvina Maud Mackey** called to rest 19th June 1987, aged 78 years.

C15-20 [space to drive].

ROW C16 [Short row starting behind **Duffy** plot in C15-6].

C16-1 [space].

C16-2 [**TAYLOR** plot]. In loving memory of **Margaret Jane**, died 17th Jan. 1932. Her husband **William John** died 14th Feb. 1960. Sons: **William James** died 31st March 1982. **Thomas George** died 3rd May 1990.

C16-3 [Plot]. In memory of **Elizabeth J. Rowe**, died 24th Jany. 1924. And **Ellen Cawthers** died 23rd April 1927. Also **Thomas H. Rowe** died 5th May 1927. And of **Lucinda Rowe,** died 6th April 1939. **Isabel Rowe** died 2nd June 1959. **William J. Rowe** died 15th Feb. 1961. **Gerard Rowe** died 2nd May 1978. **Elizabeth Rowe** 1907-1999.

C16-4 [space].

ROW C17 [Short row].

C17-1 [space].

C17-2 [**SWINDLE** plot with headstone and flower holder]. In loving memory of a dear husband and father **William John**, called home on 22nd March 1979, aged 72 years. Also his wife **Jane** called home 3rd February 1991, aged [blank] years. And their son **John Phillips** called home 26th September 1994, aged 49 years. [Flower holder]. **Swindle**. From **Rodney, Glynis, Grace** & **Pauline**.

C17-3 [space].

Transcriptions

Row C18

C18-1 [space].

C18-2 [**ARMSTRONG** plot]. In fond remembrance of **Walter Irvine**, died 31st December 1972, aged 60 years. Also his wife **Janet (Jean) Fletcher** died 5th September 2001, aged 81 years.

C18-3 [spaces].

C18-4 [**GRAHAM** plot with two facing headstones]. In loving memory of **Barton Graham** who died 29th November 1913, aged 99 years. **Barton Graham** died 1st Jan. 1974. His son **Barton** died 5th Jan. 1951. Also grandson **Stephen** died 16th Aug. 1976. **Elizabeth Jane** died 30th October 1986, aged 71 years. Erected by his children: **Sarah Ann** and **Thomas**. [2]. **Sarah Ann Graham**, 2-9-2010, aged 64.

C18-5 [Plot with two facing headstones]. In loving memory of **James Speer**, died 2nd Jany. 1913, aged 39 yrs. Erected by his widow and sisters. [2]. In loving memory of our dear father **William Speer**, died 7th Feb. 1922, aged 81 years. Also our dear mother **Isabella** died 17th November 1925, aged 74 years. Their son **William** died 2nd July 1962, age 68 yrs. Grandson **Frank** died 10th June 1977, aged 48 years. Their daughter-in-law **Sarah Jane** died 6th July 1986, aged 87 years. Erected by their children.

C18-6 [spaces and mounds].

Transcriptions

C18-7 [**ARMSTRONG** plot with pink granite headstone]. In loving memory of **Frederick Armstrong** (Letterkeen) who passed away 1st Dec. 1912, age 17 yrs. Also **Margaret Jane Armstrong** who died 13th April 1926, age 27 yrs. Their father **Henry** died 9th March 1932, aged 78 yrs. And his wife **Jane** died 5th May 1936. **Johnston** died 16th Oct. 1976, aged 89 years.

C18-8 [spaces and mounds].

C18-9 [Headstone]. Erected by **Wm. Johnston** (Mullanmeen*) in memory of his beloved wife **Martha**, died 30th March 1911, aged 48 years. Also the above named **William Johnston** died 10th December 1947, aged 82 years.

C18-10 [spaces to end of row].

ROW C19 [short row].

C19-1 [space].

C19-2 [**NOBLE** partial plot; no details].

C19-3 [spaces].

C19-4 [Fenced plot]. In loving memory of **Eleanor Wade** who died 19th June 1907, aged 74 years. **Richard Wade** who died 17th October 1910, aged 93 years.

C19-4 [spaces].

Transcriptions

ROW C20 [Last row before walkway].

C20-1 [spaces].

C20-2 [**NOBLE** plot]. (Drumnagalliagh). Precious memories of a dear father and mother: **Edward** died 7th September 1987, aged 84 years. **Elizabeth** died 12th December 1987, aged 89 years.

C20-3 [Plot]. In loving memory of the **Noble** Family (Gortnagullion).

C20-4 [spaces].

C20-5 [Plot with flat stone]. In memory of **James Johnston**, J.P. (Aghagrefin*), died 18th August 1900, aged 58 years. Also **Lena**, wife of Dr. **Johnston**, died 11th Sept. 1972. Dr. **James Percy Johnston** died 8th Dec. 1978, aged 98 years.

C20-6 [spaces and mounds].

C20-7 [Headstone with lead letters missing]. In loving memory of **Andrew Loane** (Montiaghroe*), who died 18th August 1902, aged 34 years. **Robert Loane**, 1865-1924. His wife **Mary Jane**, 1872-1926. Their sons: **Robert John**, 1905-1959. And **Christopher**, 1898-1971. **Christopher**'s wife **Annie** (*nee* **Watson**) 1901-1980. **Robert John**'s wife **Lily** (*nee* **Watson**) 1914-2012.

C20-8 [spaces].

Transcriptions

C20-9 [Headstone]. In loving memory of **James Brandon**, died 12th Sept. 1902, aged 84 years. And his wife **Sarah Brandon** died 11th March 1911, aged 75 years.

C20-10 [Headstone facing opposite direction]. Erected by **Martha McCutcheon** (Tievaveeny*) in loving memory of her husband **Charles McCutcheon**, died 22nd Feb. 1932, aged 92 years. Also the above **Martha McCutcheon** died 11th August 1955, aged 83 years.

C20-11 [Plot with low iron railing]. Erected by **John Johnston** (Skea) in loving memory of his wife **Jane** who departed this life 20th February 1904, aged 65 years. Also the above **John Johnston** died 2nd Oct. 1905, aged 73 years.

C20-12 [Headstone]. Erected by **Maggie Johnston** in loving memory of her father **John Johnston** (Feddans), who died April 19th 1905, aged 77 years.

C20-13 [spaces and mounds].

C20-14 [**WOODS** plot; no details].

C20-15 [space to end of row].

Walkway

Transcriptions

SECTION D

ROW D1

D1-1 [spaces].

D1-2 [**JOHNSTON** plot]. In loving memory of a dear wife and mother **Eileen**, died 29th May 2003, aged 83 years. Also a dear husband, father and grandfather **Percy**, died 12th March 2012, aged 90 years.

D1-3 [Plot with heart-shaped headstone]. In loving memory of a dear mother & grandmother **Amelia Williams**, died 08-01-2007, aged 90 years.

D1-4 [**NOBLE** plot with headstone and book–shaped plaque]. In loving memory of a dear husband and father **John James (Ivan)**, died 18th May 1995, aged 49 years. [Plaque]. Love **Liz, Keith, Karen, Steven, Stephanie**, grandchildren & families.

D1-5 [**McCUTCHEON** plot]. In loving memory of a dear wife **Dorothy Jane**, died 26th January 1995, aged 69 years. Also her husband **John** died 25th January 2003, aged 80 years.

D1-6 [**NOBLE** plot]. Precious memories of a dear husband and father. **Albert Johnston** died 6th April 1993, aged 70 years.

D1-7 [**NOBLE** plot]. In loving memory of a dear husband and father **John Alexander**, died 12th May 1994, aged 65 years.

D1-8 [**BRADY** partial plot]. In loving memory of a dear husband **William John**, died 16th November 1993, aged 80 years. And his brother **George** died 16th October 1999, aged 80 years.

D1-9 [**VANCE** partial plot]. In loving memory of **James (Jim)**, died 3rd July 1991. Also his wife **Annie Isobel** died 4th March 1993. Baby **Nathan** died 5th October 1995.

D1-10 [**CLARK** partial plot]. In loving memory of (Baby) **Andrew**, died 23rd July 1990.

D1-11 [**HILLIARD** headstone]. In loving memory of **Thomas Robert Charles (Tommy)**, departed this life 20th September 1991, aged 51 years).

D1-12 [**CHITTICK** plot]. In loving memory of a dear husband and father. **Archibald** died 1st February 1994, aged 93 years. And his wife **Elizabeth** died 1st March 1996, aged 85 years.

D1-13 [Narrow plot]. Rev. **J.G.B. Roycroft**, 1926-2004, loving father and grandfather.

D1-14 [space].

Transcriptions

D1-15 [**HARRON** plot]. Treasured memories of a precious daughter, grand-daughter and niece. **Kayleigh Elizabeth Eva** died 27th July 1999, aged 14 months.

D1-16 [**BARTON** plot]. In loving memory of **Cecil Hubert**, died 9th March 2003, aged 90 years.

D1-17 [Space with **OGLE** flower holder].

D1-18 [**NOBLE** plot]. In loving memory of **Mary Ann Jane**, died 5th August 2001, aged 82 years. Also her husband **Hamilton** died 25th February 2003, aged 86 years. And his brother **Edward Henry** died 20th April 2003, aged 82 years.

D1-19 [**McFARLAND** partial plot]. In loving memory of **Ivy**, died 31st August 2002, aged 71 years. Also her husband **Joseph** died 7th March 2004, aged 90 years.

D1-20 [**McFARLAND** headstone]. In loving memory of **Robert**, died 20th December 2005, aged 96 years.

D1-21 [space].

D1-22 [**LUCAS** plot]. In loving memory of a devoted wife, mother, sister and grandmother, **Oriel Georgina** passed away 4th January 2012, aged 63.

D1-23 [spaces to end of row].

Transcriptions

ROW D2

D2-1 [spaces].

D2-2 [**THOMPSON** partial plot]. In loving memory of a dear husband, father and grandfather **Stanley**, died 1st May 2011, aged 65 years.

D2-3 [Partial plot]. In loving memory of **Gertie Wilson** (*nee* **Noble**), a wonderful mum, sister and friend, died 14th April 2011, aged 57 years.

D2-4 [**ALLEN** plot]. In loving memory of a beloved husband, father, grandfather and great grandfather **Alex**, called home 3rd December 2014, aged 83 years.

D2-5 [**McCUTCHEON** partial plot]. (Gortnaree). In loving memory of a dear sister **Mary Jane**, died 28th November 1997, aged 79 years. Also her brother **Thomas** died 14th April 2002, aged 87 years.

D2-6 [space].

D2-7 [**CALDWELL** headstone]. In loving memory of a dear husband and father **Jim**, died 20th April 1995, aged 56 years.

D2-8 [**CALDWELL** headstone]. Precious memories of a dearly loved daughter & sister **Jennifer Violet (Jenny)**, died 17th July 2010, aged 16 years.

Transcriptions

D2-9 [Partial plot with white headstone]. In loving memory of **John Thompson**, B.E.M., (Kesh), who died 25th Feb. 1997, aged 65 years.

D2-10 [many spaces].

D2-11 [**JOHNSTON** partial plot]. In loving memory of **Francis James**, died 26th August 2003, aged 63 years. And his loving wife **Joan** died 8th August 2013, aged 63 years.

D2-12 [spaces].

D2-13 [**RUNACRES** partial plot]. In loving memory of a dear husband **Denis**, died 14-03-2014, aged 73 years.

D2-14 [**ALLEN** plot]. In loving memory of a dear wife, mother and grandmother **Violet Elizabeth**, died 4th April 2004, aged 70 years.

D2-15 [space].

D2-16 [**FITZPATRICK** plot]. In loving memory of **Acheson Fitzpatrick**, died 9th July 2004, aged 92 years, a beloved uncle.

D2-17 [**ARMSTRONG** plot]. In loving memory of a devoted husband, father and granda **Alexander**, died 29th January 2005, aged 77 years.

D2-18 [**LOANE** plot]. Treasured memories of a wonderful loving husband and father **Roger Alexander** died 5-11-08, aged 63 years.

Transcriptions

D2-19 [**HURLEY** plot]. In loving memory of a dear husband and father **Christopher Gerald**, died 3rd November 2011, aged 70 yrs.

D2-20 [space].

D2-21 [**FRAZER** plot]. In loving memory of a dear wife and mother **Hazel Yvonne**, died 13th September 2013, aged 45 years.

D2-22 [spaces to end of row].

SECTION E

ROW E1

E1 [**BROGAN** headstone]. In loving memory of **John**, passed away 15th July 2011. His wife **Margaret** passed away 17th December 2013.

Memorials Within Church

M1 To the Glory of God and to commemorate **George Vaughan** Esquire, 1693-1763. By his generosity the Charitable Charter School (1787-1934), and this church were erected. School land was used to establish the Vaughan Agricultural Institute, 1936-1973. Proceeds from the sale of his estate support the charitable work of the Vaughan Trust. Erected by the Vaughan Trustees in 2014.

M2 To the Glory of God and in honour of Constable **Roberts Keys**, R.U.C., who gave his life in the faithful execution of his duty at Belleek on 26th November 1972. Erected by his son **Robert**.

M3 Honour Roll, Parish of Drumkeeran [WW1]

Rev. W.F. Morris, MC, CF	Ulster Division, Royal Irish Rifles
Capt. Thos. Milligan, MC	Royal Field Artillery
Lt. Harry Hunt	Royal Engineers
William Grimsley	Royal Field Artillery
John Johnston	Royal Garrison Artillery
William Cuthertson	Royal Garrison Artillery
Sgt. Johnston Armstrong, MM	North Irish Horse
Johnston Armstrong	North Irish Horse
Sampson Trotter	North Irish Horse
Tom Johnston	North Irish Horse
Geo. Milligan	North Irish Horse
Geo. Thompson	North Irish Horse
Jack Armstrong	Inniskilling Dragoons
Edward McCartney	Inniskilling Dragoons
William Ramsey	Inniskilling Dragoons
James Marshall	Princess Royal Dragoons
Thomas Trotter	Irish Guards
Sgt. James Brown	Royal Air Force
John Chittick	Inniskilling Fusiliers

Transcriptions

Charles Thompson	Inniskilling Fusiliers
Robert Irvine	Inniskilling Fusiliers
Benjamin Graham*	Inniskilling Fusiliers
James Graham*	Inniskilling Fusiliers
Herbert Cornell	Inniskilling Fusiliers
John Little	Inniskilling Fusiliers
David Caldwell	Inniskilling Fusiliers
William Allen*	Inniskilling Fusiliers
Robert Armstrong	Military Police
Sgt. Thos. W. Johnston, DCM	Machine Gun Corps
R.L. Spence	Army Service Corps
Tom Irvine	Army Service Corps
John Johnston*	Australian Contingent
Alexander Loane	Canadians
Thos. Jas. Ramsey	Canadians
Joseph Armstrong	Wiltshire Regiment
Wm. Jas. Armstrong	Wiltshire Regiment
Barton Allen	American Army
Tom Allen	Canadians
William Verner	Royal Irish Rifles
* = killed	

M4 [Plaque]. In memory of 2nd Lieutenant **John Morris**, born in this Parish of Tubrid (son of Very Reverend Dean **W.F. Morris**, MA, MC, CF, Curate of this parish 1905-1919 and Rector 1921-1932). Royal Army Ordnance Corps, killed in action commanding A. Platoon First

Worchester Regiment, Malaya, 27th May 1951, age 21 years.

M5 [Stained glass window]. Dedicated to the Glory of God and in loving memory of **William John** and **Susan Stevenson**. Presented by their son and daughters.

M6 [Brass plaque]. To the Glory of God the electric lighting system has been installed by the **Duffy** family in loving memory of their niece **Hazel Elizabeth Francis** [sic] **Martin** who departed this life on June 4th 1954.

M7 Erected by Mrs. **Frances Tuthill** to the memory of her beloved husband the Revd. **Hugh Tuthill**, 20 years Rector of this parish, who departed this life the 27th of Nov. 1822, aged 72 years.

M8 Board with collected brass dedicatory plaques.

M8-1 To the Glory of God, presented by **Thomas McCutcheon**, 19 Sept. 1997.

M8-2 The electric motor for the bell was donated in memory of **Thomas A. Johnston** (Skea) by his wife and family.

M8-3 To the Glory of God in memory of **Jim Caldwell**, the tape recorder was presented by his wife **Pearl** and family, 22 September 1995.

Transcriptions

M8-4 To the Glory of God and in loving memory of **Angelina Hester Moore** these doors were donated by her husband **Robert**, Christmas 1983.

M8-5 The front entrance gates were presented by the **Ogle** family (Dromore Little) in memory of **Elizabeth Ogle**, died 22nd October 1950 and her son **David Ogle**, died 2nd May 1967.

M8-6 To the glory of God and in loving memory of **Robert Moore** the amplification system was donated by his grandson **Dale Lyttle**, December 1990.

M8-7 Floodlighting donated by Mr. & Mrs. **Andy Clarke** in loving memory of Baby **Andrew** who died 23rd July 1990. Dedicated to the Glory of God by Rev. **J.G.B. Roycroft.**

M9 [Plaque]. 1920 – 1970. Ulster Special Constabulary. In grateful memory of all members who served in the Tubrid Sub-District Platoon. Also Wor[shipful] Bro. Canon **Walter A. Stack**, M.A., D.M., the first B Special to join in Co. Fermanagh, Rector of Tubrid Parish Church, 1895-1921.

Transcriptions

Key to Index of Names

Each person mentioned on the gravestones or memorials has been included in the index. This might result in a person being listed more than once in the index because they might have erected a monument for a family member, but were buried under another one. Each person's name has been keyed to his/her location in the cemetery; for example, C2-3, meaning C section, row 2, number 3.

When a woman has been identified as married, her surname has been *italicized*.

Where there is uncertainty about ages or dates the numbers have been followed by a ? mark.

Key

Index of Names and Locations

	A	B	C	D
1	**Surname**	**Names**	**Death**	**Location**
2	Aiken	Esther	1921	C12-3
3	Aiken	Sidney	1920	C12-3
4	Aiken	Thomas		C12-3
5	Aiken			C7-5
6	Allen	Alex	2014	D2-4
7	Allen	Barton		M-3
8	Allen	Christopher	1989	C1-5
9	*Allen*	Ellen	1900	C1-5
10	*Allen*	Emily	1970	C1-5
11	Allen	John	1900	C1-5
12	*Allen*	Phoebe	1947	C1-5
13	Allen	Samuel	1916	C1-5
14	Allen	Tom		M-3
15	*Allen*	Violet Elizabeth	2004	D2-14
16	Allen	William	1920	C1-5
17	Allen	William	1916	C1-5
18	Allen	William		M-3
19	Allen			C10-4
20	*Allingham*	Catherine	1932	C10-7
21	Allingham	Charlotte	1956	C12-5
22	*Allingham*	Elizabeth Jane	1928	C12-5
23	Allingham	Emily		C10-7
24	Allingham	Frances	1919	C12-5
25	Allingham	Frances Jane	1945	C12-5
26	Allingham	George	1931	C10-7
27	Allingham	Mary Alice	1956	C12-5
28	Allingham	Sidney	1917	C12-5
29	*Anderson*	Elizabeth	1925	C15-6
30	Armstrong	Alexander	1963	C5-10
31	Armstrong	Alexander	2005	D2-17
32	Armstrong	Annie	1922	C13-15
33	Armstrong	Catherine	1890	C2-5

Index of Names and Locations

	A	B	C	D
1	Surname	Names	Death	Location
34	Armstrong	Colin	1970	C8-3
35	Armstrong	Edith Maud	1998	C7-2
36	*Armstrong*	Elizabeth	1956	C5-10
37	*Armstrong*	Faith	1981	C13-15
38	Armstrong	Frederick	1912	C18-7
39	Armstrong	George	1941	C5-10
40	Armstrong	Henry	1933	C13-15
41	Armstrong	Henry	1932	C18-7
42	Armstrong	Irvine	1912	C12-9
43	Armstrong	Irvine	1965	C12-9
44	*Armstrong*	Isabella	1951	C8-3
45	Armstrong	Isabella	1934	C13-15
46	Armstrong	Isobel	1962	C5-10
47	Armstrong	Jack		M-3
48	Armstrong	James	1959	C2-5
49	Armstrong	James	1944	C8-3
50	Armstrong	James	1963	C8-3
51	*Armstrong*	Jane	1936	C18-7
52	*Armstrong*	Janet (Jean)	2001	C18-2
53	Armstrong	John	1972	C5-10
54	Armstrong	John		M-3
55	Armstrong	John Alexander	2014	C5-3
56	Armstrong	Johnston	1968	C5-3
57	Armstrong	Johnston	1976	C18-7
58	Armstrong	Johnston		M-3
59	Armstrong	Johnston		M-3
60	Armstrong	Joseph		M-3
61	Armstrong	Margaret Jane	1926	C18-7
62	*Armstrong*	Mary	1970	C5-3
63	*Armstrong*	May	1990	C8-3
64	Armstrong	Robert		M-3
65	*Armstrong*	Sarah Ann	1974	C2-5

Index of Names and Locations

	A	B	C	D
1	**Surname**	**Names**	**Death**	**Location**
66	*Armstrong*	Susan	1918	C12-9
67	*Armstrong*	Susanna	1971	C7-2
68	Armstrong	Thomas	1932	C2-5
69	Armstrong	Thomas William J.	1998	C2-5
70	Armstrong	Walter Irvine	1972	C18-2
71	Armstrong	William James	1979	C13-15
72	Armstrong	William John	2006	C7-2
73	Armstrong	Wm. Jas.		M-3
74	Armstrong			C4-4
75	Armstrong			C5-6
76	Barton	Adam	1973	C6-14
77	*Barton*	Ann	1910	C12-6
78	Barton	Cecil Hubert	2003	D1-16
79	Barton	Folliott Warren	1922	C12-6
80	Barton	George	1942	C13-6
81	Barton	George	1967	C13-6
82	Barton	Harry	1982	C13-6
83	*Barton*	Isabella	1959	C6-14
84	Barton	John	1907	C3-9
85	Barton	John	1943	C7-9
86	Barton	Margaret D.	1944	C12-6
87	Barton	Martha	1940	C7-9
88	*Barton*	Rebecca	1920	C3-9
89	Barton	Sarah		C3-9
90	*Barton*	Sarah Jane	1957	C13-6
91	Barton	Thomas	1898	C12-6
92	Barton	William	1921	C3-9
93	Barton			C3-6
94	Beatty	James	1915	C15-15
95	Beatty	William John	1921	C15-15
96	*Bell*	Mary Ann	1974	C13-2
97	Bell	Thomas	1992	C13-2

Index of Names and Locations

	A	B	C	D
1	**Surname**	**Names**	**Death**	**Location**
98	Bell	Willie	1972	C13-2
99	*Boyd*	Annie	1984	C14-10
100	Boyd	Irvine	1972	C14-10
101	Boyd	John	1945	C14-10
102	Boyd	Sadie	1984	C15-12
103	*Boyd*	Sidney	1921	C14-10
104	Boyd	Thomas	1984	C14-10
105	Brady	George	1999	D1-8
106	Brady	William John	1993	D1-8
107	Brandon	Elizabeth	1990	C9-8
108	Brandon	James	1902	C20-9
109	Brandon	John	1932	C9-8
110	Brandon	Mary Brandon	1934	C9-8
111	*Brandon*	Sarah	1911	C20-9
112	Brandon	William	1989	C9-8
113	Brimstone	James	1941	C5-9
114	Brimstone	James Alexander	1983	C5-9
115	*Brimstone*	Mary W.W.	1975	C5-9
116	Brogan	John	2011	E1
117	*Brogan*	Magaret	2013	E1
118	Brown	James	1966	C6-10
119	Brown	James		M-3
120	Brown	James Frederick	1986	C15-18
121	*Brown*	Mary Annabella	1957*	C6-10
122	Brown	Maud Elizabeth	2007	C15-18
123	Brown	Thomas	1966	C6-10
124	Caldwell	David		M-3
125	Caldwell	Jennifer Violet	2010	D2-8
126	Caldwell	Jim	1995	D2-7
127	Caldwell	Jim		M8-3
128	*Caldwell*	Pearl		M8-3
129	Cawthers	Ellen	1927	C16-3

Index of Names and Locations

	A	B	C	D
1	**Surname**	**Names**	**Death**	**Location**
130	*Chittick*	Annie	1929	C9-9
131	Chittick	Archibald	1997	C13-6
132	Chittick	Archibald	1994	D1-12
133	*Chittick*	Christianna	1910	C12-8
134	*Chittick*	Elizabeth	1996	D1-12
135	*Chittick*	Elizabeth J.	1928	C13-6
136	*Chittick*	Elizabeth Jane	1974	C9-9
137	Chittick	George	1939	C9-9
138	Chittick	George	1942	C9-9
139	Chittick	George Alexander	1986	C9-9
140	Chittick	John		M-3
141	Chittick	John Henry	1978	C9-9
142	Chittick	Thomas	1910	C12-8
143	Chittick	William	1961	C13-6
144	Chittick	William Sampson	1980	C13-6
145	Clark	Andrew	1990	D1-10
146	Clarke	Andrew	1990	M8-7
147	Clarke	Andy		M8-7
148	Connell	Herbert		M-3
149	Cutherbertson	Andrew	1944	C13-19
150	Cutherbertson	Elizabeth	1974	C13-18
151	*Cutherbertson*	Frances	1942	C13-19
152	*Cutherbertson*	Jane	1929	C13-18
153	Cutherbertson	John	1929	C13-19
154	Cutherbertson	Robert	1979	C13-18
155	Cutherbertson	William	1929	C13-18
156	Cutherbertson	William	1943	C13-18
157	Cutherbertson	William		M-3
158	Dick	Christopher	1955	C12-12
159	Dick	Kathleen Mildred	1980	C12-12
160	*Dick*	Rachel Jane	1935	C12-12
161	Dick	William John	2000	C12-12

	A	B	C	D
1	**Surname**	**Names**	**Death**	**Location**
162	Duffy	Elizabeth	1974	C15-6
163	*Duffy*	Frances	1915	C15-6
164	Duffy	Hiram	1918	C15-6
165	Duffy	Mary Jane	1975	C15-6
166	Duffy	Robert	1944	C15-6
167	Duffy	William John	1971	C15-6
168	Duffy			M6
169	*Dundas*	Edith M.	1961	C11-4
170	Dundas	Robert C.	1937	C11-4
171	Farrell			C7-15B
172	Farrell			C8-4
173	Fitzpatrick	Acheson	2004	D2-16
174	Fitzpatrick	Alexander	1986	C12-7
175	*Fitzpatrick*	Martha	1899	C2-2
176	Fitzpatrick	Susan	1954	C12-7
177	Fitzpatrick	William	1894	C2-2
178	Fitzpatrick	William James	1958	C12-7
179	*Forde*	Rebecca	1933	C9-12
180	Fraser	John Huston	1926	C12-6
181	Frazer	Alexander	1935	C9-12
182	*Frazer*	Hazel Yvonne	2013	D2-21
183	Frazer	Irvine	1943	C9-12
184	Frazer	Isobel	1967	C5-4
185	Frazer	James	1984	C9-12
186	*Frazer*	Margaret	1958	C9-12
187	*Frazer*	Mary Elizabeth	1967	C5-4
188	Frazer	Samuel Albert	1985	C5-4
189	Frazer	William	1966	C9-12
190	Gibson	Emily	1980	C3-8
191	Gibson	Frederick	1984	C3-8
192	*Gibson*	Margaret	1964	C3-8
193	Gibson	William	1949	C3-8

Index of Names and Locations

	A	B	C	D
1	**Surname**	**Names**	**Death**	**Location**
194	Gilmore			C5-12
195	Graham	Ann		C18-4
196	Graham	Barton	1913	C18-4
197	Graham	Barton	1974	C18-4
198	Graham	Barton	1951	C18-4
199	Graham	Benjamin		M-3
200	Graham	Elizabeth Jane	1986	C18-4
201	*Graham*	Evelyn	1971	C5-8
202	*Graham*	Helena	1942	C5-8
203	Graham	James		M-3
204	Graham	John	1966	C5-8
205	Graham	Sarah		C18-4
206	Graham	Sarah Ann	2010	C18-4
207	Graham	Stephen	1976	C18-4
208	Graham	Thomas		C18-4
209	Graham	William John	2000	C5-8
210	Grimsley	Annie	1993	C3-2
211	*Grimsley*	Elizabeth	1972	C3-2
212	Grimsley	William	1959	C3-2
213	Grimsley	William	1980	C3-2
214	Grimsley	William		M-3
215	Hargreaves	James Robert	1985	C10-11
216	Hargreaves	John	1985	C10-11
217	Harron	Kayleigh Elizabeth	1999	D1-15
218	Hart	Henry George	1964	C12-6
219	*Hart*	Margaret	1979	C12-6
220	Hart	William Folliott	2010	C12-6
221	Hilliard	Thomas Robert C.	1991	D1-11
222	Humphries	Henry		C7-13A
223	*Humphries*	Sarah	1944	C7-13A
224	Hunt	Harry		M-3
225	Hurley	Christopher Gerald	2011	D2-19

Index of Names and Locations

	A	B	C	D
1	**Surname**	**Names**	**Death**	**Location**
226	Irvine	Robert		M-3
227	Irvine	Tom		M-3
228	*Johnston*	Alice	1956	C6-5
229	*Johnston*	Catherine	1973	C5-15B
230	*Johnston*	Eileen	2003	D1-2
231	*Johnston*	Elizabeth Jane	1979	C10-11
232	Johnston	Eva	1979	C10-11
233	Johnston	Francis James	2003	D2-11
234	Johnston	George	1967	C5-15B
235	Johnston	George	1950	C10-11
236	Johnston	George	1979	C14-2
237	Johnston	Henrietta Mary	1937	C10-11
238	Johnston	James	1964	C6-5
239	Johnston	James	1925	C10-11
240	Johnston	James		C15-13
241	Johnston	James	1900	C20-5
242	Johnston	James Percy	1978	C20-5
243	*Johnston*	Jane	1933	C9-11
244	*Johnston*	Jane	1904	C20-11
245	*Johnston*	Joan	2013	D2-11
246	Johnston	John	1905	C20-11
247	Johnston	John	1905	C20-12
248	Johnston	John		M-3
249	*Johnston*	Lena	1972	C20-5
250	Johnston	Maggie		C20-12
251	*Johnston*	Margaret	1934	C9-11
252	*Johnston*	Martha	1911	C18-9
253	Johnston	Martha Jean	1931	C10-11
254	*Johnston*	Mary Jane	1920	C10-11
255	*Johnston*	Nancy	1943	C10-11
256	Johnston	Percy	2012	D1-2
257	Johnston	Richard James	1980	C10-11

Index of Names and Locations

	A	B	C	D
1	**Surname**	**Names**	**Death**	**Location**
258	Johnston	Robert Edward	1923	C10-11
259	Johnston	Sarah	1948	C11-7
260	*Johnston*	Sarah	1914	C15-13
261	Johnston	Thomas A.		M8-2
262	Johnston	Thos. W.		M-3
263	Johnston	Tom		M-3
264	Johnston	William	1922	C9-11
265	Johnston	William	1920	C15-13
266	Johnston	William James	2004	C5-15B
267	Johnston	Wm.		C9-11
268	Johnston	Wm.	1947	C18-9
269	Johnston			C6-12
270	Johnston			C11-9
271	Johnston			C14-7
272	*Kennedy*	C. Joyce	2004	C5-9
273	*Keys*	Lilian	1996	C4-2
274	Keys	Robert	1972	C4-2
275	Keys	Robert	1972	M2
276	Keys	Robert		M2
277	*Kidney*	Elizabeth	1966	C5-5
278	Kidney	Richard	1966	C5-5
279	Kidney	Thomas J.	1969	C5-5
280	*Knox*	Evelyn Knox	1972	C13-11
281	Knox	Matthew Henry	1979	C13-11
282	Lennox			C7-14B
283	Leonard	Henry	1875	C2-9
284	Lewthwaite			C5-12
285	Little	John		M-3
286	Loane	Alexander		M-3
287	Loane	Andrew	1902	C20-7
288	*Loane*	Annie	1980	C20-7
289	Loane	Christopher	1952	C14-8

Index of Names and Locations

	A	B	C	D
1	**Surname**	**Names**	**Death**	**Location**
290	Loane	Christopher	1971	C20-7
291	Loane	Earnest Carson	1920	C14-8
292	*Loane*	Elizabeth Mary	1976	C15-2
293	Loane	Irvine	1960	C15-2
294	Loane	James	1985	C15-2
295	Loane	John	1983	C14-8
296	Loane	Kathleen	1979	C14-8
297	*Loane*	Lily	2012	C20-7
298	*Loane*	Mary Jane	1926	C20-7
299	Loane	Robert	1924	C20-7
300	Loane	Robert John	1959	C20-7
301	Loane	Roger Alexander	2008	D2-18
302	*Loane*	Sarah Jane	1957	C14-8
303	Loane	William	1934	C14-8
304	*Lucas*	Oriel Georgina	2012	D1-22
305	Lyttle	Dale		M8-6
306	Mackey	Louisa Irvina Maud	1987	C15-19
307	Marshall	Alfred	1997	C7-7
308	Marshall	Annie	1978	C11-11
309	Marshall	Edward	1919	C14-5
310	Marshall	Ernest J.	1987	C7-8
311	*Marshall*	Evelyn	2007	C7-7
312	Marshall	George	1985	C14-5
313	Marshall	Henry	1979	C14-5
314	Marshall	Herbert	1988	C7-7
315	*Marshall*	Isabella Margaret	2002	C14-5
316	Marshall	Isobell	1969	C11-11
317	Marshall	James		M-3
318	Marshall	John	1958	C11-11
319	Marshall	John	1932	C14-5
320	Marshall	Martha Elizabeth	1978	C14-5
321	Marshall	Mary	1901	C14-5

Index of Names and Locations

	A	B	C	D
1	**Surname**	**Names**	**Death**	**Location**
322	Marshall	Mary Jane	1961	C7-7
323	Marshall	Murial	1942	C14-5
324	Marshall	Olive	1941	C14-5
325	*Marshall*	Sarah	1929	C14-5
326	Marshall			C12-10
327	Martin	Hazel Elizabeth F.	1954	M6
328	*Martin*	Jane	1969	C6-4
329	*Martin*	Maud Evelyn	2007	C6-4
330	Martin	Robert H.	1984	C5-15B
331	Martin	Robert Henry	2005	C6-4
332	Martin	William John	1965	C6-4
333	McCartney	Alfred	1935	C10-6
334	McCartney	Edward	1976	C10-6
335	McCartney	Edward		M-3
336	McCartney	Johnston	1921	C11-7
337	*McCartney*	Letitia	1925	C11-7
338	*McCartney*	Margaret Ellen	1986	C10-6
339	*McCartney*	Rebecca	1948	C11-7
340	McCartney	Samuel Edward	2010	C10-6
341	McCartney	Wm. J.	1941	C11-7
342	McClelland	Edward	1935	C4-9
343	McClelland	Elizabeth Annabella	1968	C4-9
344	*McClelland*	Isabella	1952	C4-9
345	McClelland			C13-13
346	*McCormick*	Bessie	1916	C3-10
347	McCormick	David	1937	C15-8
348	McCormick	Elizabeth		C15-8
349	McCormick	Joe	1907	C3-10
350	*McCormick*	Mary	1925	C15-8
351	McCormick	Rose	1919	C15-8
352	McCrea	George	1941	C12-13
353	*McCrea*	Mary Jane	1968	C12-13

Index of Names and Locations

	A	B	C	D
1	Surname	Names	Death	Location
354	McCutcheon	Charles	1936	C11-8
355	McCutcheon	Charles	1932	C20-10
356	*McCutcheon*	Dorothy Jane	1995	D1-5
357	*McCutcheon*	Eliza Jane	1964	C11-8
358	*McCutcheon*	Elizabeth Jane	1967	C15-10
359	McCutcheon	John	1936	C15-10
360	McCutcheon	John	2003	D1-5
361	*McCutcheon*	Margaret	1929	C11-8
362	*McCutcheon*	Martha	1955	C20-10
363	McCutcheon	Mary Jane	1997	D2-5
364	McCutcheon	Robert	1918	C15-9
365	McCutcheon	Thomas	1924	C11-8
366	McCutcheon	Thomas	2002	D2-5
367	McCutcheon	Thomas		M8-1
368	*McFarland*	Ivy	2002	D1-19
369	McFarland	Joseph	2004	D1-19
370	McFarland	Robert	2005	D1-20
371	Milligan	Geo.		M-3
372	Milligan	Thos.		M-3
373	*Mills*	Dora	2010	C9-13
374	Mills	Joseph	1968	C9-13
375	*Mills*	Mary	1976	C9-13
376	Mills	William	1994	C9-13
377	*Moore*	Angelina Hester		M8-3
378	*Moore*	Anna Elizabeth	1989	C13-10
379	Moore	Charles	1917	C14-4
380	Moore	Daisy	1981	C7-10
381	*Moore*	Elizabeth	1953	C10-10
382	*Moore*	Elizabeth Gibson	1927	C14-4
383	Moore	Henrietta	1934	C14-4
384	*Moore*	Isabella K.	1973	C10-10
385	Moore	James	1984	C7-10

Index of Names and Locations

	A	B	C	D
1	**Surname**	**Names**	**Death**	**Location**
386	Moore	James	1929	C10-10
387	Moore	James	1986	C10-10
388	*Moore*	Mary	1988	C7-10
389	Moore	Meryn Alexander	1946	C10-10
390	*Moore*	Rebecca	1933	C7-10
391	Moore	Robert	1906	C7-10
392	Moore	Robert		M8-4
393	Moore	Robert		M8-6
394	Moore	Samuel Crawford	1993	C7-10
395	Moore	Sandra	1982	C7-10
396	Moore	Sarah	1963	C14-4
397	Moore	William	1979	C13-10
398	Moore	William	1962	C14-4
399	Morris	John	1951	M4
400	Morris	W.F.		M-3
401	Morris	W.F.		M4
402	*Morrow*	Evelyn Mary	1974	C7-3
403	Morrow	John James	1986	C7-3
404	*Morrow*	Margaret Sarah Barl	1963	C7-3
405	Morrow	William Henry	1963	C7-3
406	Morton	Chirstina Jane	1968	C6-7
407	Morton	George	1921	B1-1
408	Morton	John	1940	B1-1
409	*Morton*	Margaret	1967	B1-1
410	Morton	William	1979	C6-7
411	Noble	Albert Johnston	1993	D1-6
412	Noble	Alexander Taggart E	1940	C15-4
413	Noble	Benjamin Laurence	1947	C15-4
414	Noble	Edward	1987	C20-2
415	Noble	Edward Henry	2003	D1-18
416	*Noble*	Elizabeth	1987	C20-2
417	Noble	Hamilton	2003	D1-18

	A	B	C	D
1	**Surname**	**Names**	**Death**	**Location**
418	*Noble*	Jean		C15-4
419	Noble	John Alexander	1994	D1-7
420	Noble	John James (Ivan)	1995	D1-4
421	Noble	Karen		D1-4
422	Noble	Keith		D1-4
423	Noble	Liz		D1-4
424	*Noble*	Mary Ann Jane	2001	D1-18
425	Noble	Stephanie		D1-4
426	Noble	Steven		D1-4
427	Noble			C19-2
428	Noble			C20-3
429	Ogle	Adam	1975	C4-7
430	*Ogle*	Barbara	1910	C4-7
431	Ogle	David	1967	M8-5
432	*Ogle*	Elizabeth	1932	C4-7
433	*Ogle*	Elizabeth	1950	M8-5
434	Ogle	George	1930	C4-7
435	Ogle	Gladys Evelyn	2002	C4-7
436	Ogle			D1-17
437	Poster	A.	1842	C1-1
438	Ramsey	Thos. Jas.		M-3
439	Ramsey	William		M-3
440	Read			C13-4
441	Reid	Elizabeth	1906	C3-9
442	Richardson	Charles	1900	C2-4
443	Richardson	Kate	1901	C2-4
444	Richardson	Sarah Jane	1898	C2-4
445	Robinson	Brian	1945	C7-12
446	Robinson	Edward John	1938	C7-12
447	*Robinson*	Minnie	1990	C2-7
448	Robinson	Olive Lucy	1975	C7-12
449	Robinson	Samuel George	1986	C7-12

Index of Names and Locations

	Surname	Names	Death	Location
450	Robinson	Vivian Maud	1974	C7-12
451	Robinson	William	1986	C2-7
452	Rowe	Elizabeth	1999	C16-3
453	Rowe	Elizabeth J.	1924	C16-3
454	Rowe	Gerard	1978	C16-3
455	Rowe	Isabel	1959	C16-3
456	Rowe	Lucinda	1939	C16-3
457	Rowe	Thomas H.	1927	C16-3
458	Rowe	William J.	1961	C16-3
459	Roycroft	J.G.B.	2004	D1-13
460	Roycroft	J.G.B.		M8-7
461	Runacres	Denis	2014	D2-13
462	Seaney	Ivan	1945	B1-1
463	Seaney	John (Jack)	1967	C4-3
464	*Seaney*	Sarah (Sadie)	1992	C4-3
465	*Simms*	Mary		C3-4
466	Sims	Barton Hugh	1946	C3-3
467	Speer	Frank	1977	C18-5
468	*Speer*	Isabella	1925	C18-5
469	Speer	James	1913	C18-5
470	*Speer*	Sarah Jane	1986	C18-5
471	Speer	William	1922	C18-5
472	Speer	William	1962	C18-5
473	Spence	Ethel	1959	C11-4
474	Spence	James	1959	C11-4
475	Spence	R.L.		M-3
476	Spence	Rebecca	1938	C11-4
477	Spence	Robert L.	1932	C11-4
478	*Sproule*	Mildred	1998	C11-14
479	Sproule	Robert	1988	C11-14
480	Stack	Walter A.		M-9
481	Stedman	Jane	1847	C1-3

Index of Names and Locations

	A	B	C	D
1	**Surname**	**Names**	**Death**	**Location**
482	Stevenson	Dora	1924	C10-12
483	Stevenson	Edward	1933	C10-12
484	Stevenson	James		C13-9
485	Stevenson	John Thomas (Tom)	1951	C13-9
486	*Stevenson*	Margaret Jane	1955	C13-9
487	*Stevenson*	Martha Jane	1936	C10-12
488	*Stevenson*	Mary Ann (Minnie)	1945	C13-9
489	*Stevenson*	Susan	1972	C10-12
490	*Stevenson*	Susan		M5
491	Stevenson	William John	1975	C10-12
492	Stevenson	William John		M5
493	*Stewart*	Jane	1911	C4-6
494	Stewart	Kate Laura	1926	C4-6
495	Stewart	Thomas	1907	C4-6
496	*Swanston*	Ann Jane	1945	C10-9
497	Swanston	Elizabeth Jane	1931	C10-9
498	Swanston	William	1930	C10-9
499	*Swindall*	Lizzie	1985	C10-4
500	Swindle	Glynis		C17-2
501	Swindle	Grace		C17-2
502	*Swindle*	Jane	1991	C17-2
503	Swindle	John Phillips	1994	C17-2
504	Swindle	Pauline		C17-2
505	Swindle	Rodney		C17-2
506	Swindle	William John	1979	C17-2
507	*Taggart*	Maria H.	1915	C15-4
508	Taggart	Samuel	1969	C15-4
509	*Taylor*	Margaret Jane	1932	C16-2
510	Taylor	Thomas George	1990	C16-2
511	Taylor	William James	1982	C16-2
512	Taylor	William John	1960	C16-2
513	Thompson	Brian		C11-15

Index of Names and Locations

	A	B	C	D
1	**Surname**	**Names**	**Death**	**Location**
514	*Thompson*	Catherine		C5-14A
515	Thompson	Cecil	1978	C5-2
516	Thompson	Charles		M-3
517	*Thompson*	Elizabeth	1946	C3-3
518	*Thompson*	Elizabeth		C3-12
519	*Thompson*	Elizabeth	1968	C8-1
520	Thompson	Elsie		C11-15
521	*Thompson*	Evelyn	1979	C8-1
522	Thompson	Frank	1908	C3-3
523	Thompson	Geo.		M-3
524	Thompson	George	1959	C3-3
525	Thompson	George		C3-4
526	Thompson	Helen		C11-15
527	*Thompson*	Irene		C6-2
528	Thompson	Isaac		C3-4
529	Thompson	Jack		C5-14A
530	Thompson	James		C3-12
531	Thompson	James	1982	C3-12
532	Thompson	John		C5-14A
533	Thompson	John	1997	D2-9
534	Thompson	Linda		C11-15
535	*Thompson*	Martha	1990	C5-2
536	*Thompson*	Rose		C3-4
537	Thompson	Sandra		C11-15
538	Thompson	Sarah Jane		C3-12
539	Thompson	Stanley	2011	D2-2
540	Thompson	Thomas Edward	2013	C11-15
541	Thompson	Trevor		C11-15
542	Thompson	Victor		C6-2
543	Thompson	William John	1998	C8-1
544	Thompson	Thomas Charles	1952	C8-1
545	Trotter	Sampson		M-3

	A	B	C	D
1	**Surname**	**Names**	**Death**	**Location**
546	Trotter	Thomas		M-3
547	*Tuthill*	Frances		M7
548	Tuthill	Hugh	1822	M7
549	Tuttle	James B.	1877	A1-1
550	*Vance*	Annie Isobel	1993	D1-9
551	Vance	James (Jim)	1991	D1-9
552	Vance	Nathan	1995	D1-9
553	Vance			C4-11
554	Vaughan	George	1763	M1
555	Verner	William		M3
556	Wade	Eleanor	1907	C19-4
557	Wade	Richard	1910	C19-4
558	Walmsley	Edward	1959	C9-4
559	Walmsley	Herbert	2014	C5-7
560	Walmsley	John	1952	C5-7
561	Walmsley	Margaret	1944	C9-4
562	*Walmsley*	May	1961	C5-7
563	*Walmsley*	Sarah Anne	1946	C9-4
564	*Walmsley*	Sheila	2002	C9-4
565	Walmsley	William	2011	C9-4
566	*Williams*	Amelia	2007	D1-3
567	*Wilson*	Catherine	1989	C9-7
568	Wilson	Chalres	1974	C9-7
569	Wilson	Elizabeth	1932	C9-7
570	*Wilson*	Gertie	2011	D2-3
571	Wilson	Mervyn James	2004	C9-7
572	Wilson	Raymond Charles	1967	C9-7
573	Wilson	Robert John	1998	C9-7
574	*Wilson*			C9-6
575	*Woods*	Letitia	1988	C6-8
576	Woods	William Henry	1977	C6-8
577	Woods			C20-14

Old and New Irish Genealogy Series Titles

County Antrim

Racavan Burying Ground, Racavan Parish; 895 names. ISBN 978-1-927357-66-8. 2020

County Donegal

Finner Cemetery, Bundoran, Inishmacsaint Parish; 1008 names from Donegal and Leitrim. ISBN 978-1-927357-34-7. 2012

St. Anne's Church of Ireland Cemetery, Ballyshannon, Kilbarron Parish; 1217 names. ISBN 978-1-927357-52-1. 2016

County Fermanagh

Aghalurcher Parish

Holy Cross Roman Catholic Cemetery, Lisnaskea; 1240 names. ISBN 978-1-927357-64-4. 2019

Holy Trinity Church of Ireland Cemetery, Lisnaskea; 1296 names. ISBN 978-1-927357-63-7. 2019

Maguiresbridge Church of Ireland Cemetery; 516 names. ISBN 978-1-927357-40-8. 2014

Maguiresbridge Methodist Cemetery; 343 names. ISBN 978-1-927357-41-5. 2014

Maguiresbridge Presbyterian Cemetery; 206 names. ISBN 978-1-927357-42-2. 2014

St. Mary's Roman Catholic Cemetery, Maguiresbridge; 1296 names. ISBN 978-1-927357-68-2. 2020

Aghavea Parish

A Comprehensive Index of the Aghavea Church of Ireland Parish Registers, 1815-1912; over 8300 entries from Aghavea and Aghalurcher parishes. ISBN 978-1-927357-61-3. 2018

Aghavea Church of Ireland Cemetery; 1118 names. ISBN 978-1-927357-38-5. 2013

St. Mary's Roman Catholic Churchyard and Carrickyheenan Road Cemetery, Brookeborough; 692 names. ISBN 978-1-927357-65-1. 2019

Irish Genealogy Series

Boho Parish

Boho Church of Ireland Parish Register; 572 entries ISBN 978-0-9781764-2-6. 2006

Boho Church of Ireland Cemetery; 245 names from Fermanagh and Cavan. ISBN 978-0-9781764-6-4. 2008

St. Faber's Roman Catholic Cemetery; 757 names. ISBN 978-1-927357-01-09. 2011

Cleenish Parish

A Comprehensive Index of the Bellanaleck Church of Ireland Parish Registers (1845-1912); over 742 entries from Fermanagh and Cavan. (CD-ROM) ISBN 978-1-927357-49-1. 2015

Bellanaleck Church of Ireland Cemetery; 624 names. ISBN 978-0-9812063-7-0. 2011

Lisbellaw Church of Ireland Churchyard; 431 names. ISBN 978-1-927357-10-1. 2012

Lisbellaw Presbyterian Cemetery; 110 names. ISBN 978-1-927357-39-2. 2013

Mullaghdun Church of Ireland Cemetery; 354 names. ISBN 978-0-9812063-6-3. 2011

A Comprehensive Index of the Mullaghdun Church of Ireland Cleenish Parish Registers (1819-1912); over 2770 entries from Fermanagh and Cavan. ISBN 978-1-927357-35-4. 2013

St. Joseph's Roman Catholic Cemetery, Mullaghdun; 414 names. ISBN 978-1-927357-13-2. 2012

St. Patrick's Holy Well Cemetery, Belcoo; 784 names. ISBN 978-1-927357-58-3. 2017

Templerushin (Holy Well) Graveyard, Belcoo; 82 names ISBN 978-1-927357-57-6. 2017

St. Mary's Catholic Cemetery, Arney; 688 names. ISBN 978-1-927357-78-1. 2025

Derrybrusk Parish

St. Michael's Church of Ireland Cemetery; 393 names. ISBN 978-1-927357-59-0. 2018

Devenish Parish

A Comprehensive Index of the Devenish Church of Ireland Parish Registers; over 6300 entries. ISBN 978-0-9812063-9-4. 2011

Irish Genealogy Series

St. Patrick's Roman Catholic Cemetery, Derrygonnelly; 713 names. ISBN 978-0-9812063-2-5. 2010

Garrison Church of Ireland Cemetery; 304 names from Fermanagh, Leitrim, and Donegal. ISBN 978-0-9781764-7-1. 2008

St. Molaise Church of Ireland Cemetery, Monea; 905 names. ISBN 978-1-927357-00-2. 2012

Monea Roman Catholic Cemetery; 315 names. ISBN 978-0-9869627-4-5. 2011

Drumkeeran Parish

Colaghty Church of Ireland and Tirwinny Methodist Cemeteries; 615 names. ISBN 978-1-927357-75-0. 2025

Tubrid Church of Ireland Graveyard; updated. 575 names. ISBN 978-1-927357-77-4. 2025

Enniskillen Parish

Enniskillen Poor Law Union, Outdoor Relief Register Index: 1847-1899; about 3000 entries from Fermanagh, Tyrone and Cavan. ISBN 978-0-9781764-1-9. 2009

Irish Genealogy Series

Memorials in the Enniskillen Presbyterian Church; 110 names. ISBN 978-1-927357-67-5. 2020

Mount Lourdes Convent Cemetery, Enniskillen; over 2000 names. ISBN 978-1-927357-56-9. 2017

Inishmacsaint Parish

A Comprehensive Index to the Inishmacsaint Church of Ireland Parish Registers, Counties Fermanagh and Donegal (1800-1912); contains over 12,000 entries for Fermanagh, Donegal and Leitrim. ISBN 978-1-927357-55-2. 2016

Benmore Church of Ireland Cemetery; 613 names. ISBN 978-0-9781764-4-0. 2012

Old Derrygonnelly Churchyard; 332 names. ISBN 978-0-9781764-8-8. 2009

Garrison Roman Catholic Cemetery; 1050 names. ISBN 978-0-9812063-0-1. 2009

Slavin Church of Ireland Cemetery; 209 names from Fermanagh and Donegal. ISBN 978-1-927357-19-4. 2012

Three Old Inishmacsaint Parish Graveyards: Inishmacsaint Island, Carrick and Old Slavin; 129 names. ISBN 978-0-9869627-1-4. 2011

St. John the Baptist Roman Catholic Cemetery; 595 names. ISBN 978-1-927357-07-01. 2012

Magheracross Parish

Sydare Methodist Cemetery; 1247 names from Fermanagh, Tyrone and Donegal. ISBN 978-0-9781764-9-5. 2008

Two Magheracross Parish Burial Grounds: Old Magheracross Graveyard and the Ballina-mallard Church of Ireland Churchyard; 588 names from Fermanagh and Tyrone. ISBN 978-0-9812063-4-9. 2010

Magheraculmoney Parish

A Comprehensive Index of the St. Mary's Ardess Church of Ireland, Magheraculmoney Parish Registers, County Fermanagh, 1763-1918; 15,630 entries for Fermanagh and Tyrone. ISBN 978-1-927357-71-2. 2021

Edenclaw Catholic Cemetery, Ederney; 579 names. ISBN 978-1-927357-76-7. 2025

Rossorry Parish

Rossorry Parish Cemeteries; 1250 names. ISBN 978-0-9781764-0-2. 2009

Trory Parish

Killadeas Church of Ireland Cemetery; 283 names. ISBN 978-1-927357-04-0. 2012

St. Michael's Church of Ireland Cemetery; 320 names. ISBN 978-0-9812063-1-8. 2009

County Leitrim

Kiltyclogher Church of Ireland Churchyard, Cloonclare Parish; 20 names from Leitrim and Fermanagh. ISBN 978-1-927357-70-5. 2020

Old Rossinver Graveyard, Rossinver Parish; 1073 names from Leitrim and Fermanagh. ISBN 978-1-927357-50-7. 2016

Irish Genealogy Series

County Tyrone

St. John's Church of Ireland Churchyard, Fivemiletown, Clogher Parish; 1379 names from Tyrone and Fermanagh. ISBN 978-1-927357-16-3. 2012

St. Joseph's Catholic Cemetery, Fivemiletown, Clogher Parish; 432 names. (in production).

County Wicklow

Old Kilmurry Roman Catholic Cemetery, Newcastle Parish; 187 names. ISBN 978-1-927357-37-8. 2013

For information on where you can obtain any of the preceding titles contact KinFolk Finders by email or phone.

Email: kinfolkfinders154@gmail.com

Phone: 1-519-294-0728.

www.ingramcontent.com/pod-product-compliance
Lightning Source LLC
Chambersburg PA
CBHW061248230426

43663CB00021B/2943